This gift
provided by:

The
Seattle
Public
Library
Foundation

SUPPORTSPL.ORG

D0955318

Praise for *The Awesome Human Project*

"Abounds with simple, practical tools to build emotional fitness, learn to embrace ourselves (and our awesomeness) wholeheartedly, and to leave the 'shoulds' behind so we can joyously revel in the 'coulds.'"

MELISSA BERNSTEIN   cofounder and chief creative officer, Melissa & Doug

"An inspiring blueprint sharing Nataly's compelling personal journey and tactical ways to redirect your mind towards meaning, purpose, and fulfillment."

TIFFANY SHLAIN   Emmy-nominated filmmaker, founder of the Webby Awards, and bestselling author of *24/6: The Power of Unplugging One Day a Week*

"Just like practice in sports, *The Awesome Human Project* is hard work but rewarding. And Nataly is there like an awesome coach, dusting us off when we stumble, giving us encouragement and motivation, and supporting us on our next attempt."

JONATHAN BECHER   president, San Jose Sharks

"We've somehow been convinced that a life of busyness and struggle is the only way to live. Through self-care and self-compassion, *The Awesome Human Project* shows us another way is possible."

JEN FISHER   chief well-being officer, Deloitte

"Part self-help, part science, and part workbook, *The Awesome Human Project* offers the perfect combination of tools to help any busy professional step away from the overwhelm of everyday life and chart their way out of the chaos."

STACEY HOIN   chief human resources officer, Guardian Life Insurance

"*The Awesome Human Project* is a generous and practical guide to letting go of struggle and being your best self—from someone who truly understands what it means to build a happy life from the ground up."

INGRID FETELL LEE   author of *Joyful* and founder of The Aesthetics of Joy

"Is it possible to recommend a book to all humans? Because if so, I would absolutely recommend *The Awesome Human Project* to any human who interacts with other humans and the world around them. The lessons and practices in *The Awesome Human Project* will help me on my journey to becoming a better leader, colleague, professional, wife, mother, sister, friend, and person."

KERRI PALAMARA MCGRATH, MD   primary care physician and director of The Center for Physician Well-being at Massachusetts General Hospital

"We are in the middle of a human revolution. There has been a much-needed shift, particularly in the workplace, toward embracing the importance of being fully human and taking care of one's mental health and well-being. Nataly provides a blueprint on how to train your mind and be the best version of yourself. Human connection, kindness, and gratitude are not just nice-to-haves. They are fundamentally important on the path toward greater meaning, purpose, happiness, and a better you."

ERIC MOSLEY   CEO of Workhuman

"Each time I read Nataly's work or hear her speak, I am reminded of the power of mindset. *The Awesome Human Project* is no exception. Readers will find themselves both championed and challenged by the author, who calls us to examine and retrain our thinking. Grounded in real experiences and key neuroscientific insights, it is a pragmatic and thought-provoking guide to achieve what most find illusive—greater joy."

NOELLE EDER   global chief information officer, Cigna

"You can't give what you don't have' has become my new mantra thanks to Nataly Kogan. It has never been more important for us, as leaders, to model self-care. That's where this book comes in, distilling Nataly's engaging and effective teaching so that we can build happier, more sustainable lives. If you've gritted your teeth through the past year and wondered how long your stamina can hold out, please read this book!"

PEGGY NORTHROP   CEO, Watermark

"This is the book our world needs right now. Like a supportive friend, but one who knows when you need some tough love, Nataly guides you on a meaningful journey to embrace your full awesome self so you can work and live with more joy and purpose. *The Awesome Human Project* is one you'll want to roll up your sleeves and DO, not just read."

FRAN HAUSER   startup investor, keynote speaker, and bestselling author of *The Myth of the Nice Girl*

"What could be better than being an awesome human? Obviously, nothing! What's a close second? The book you're holding. Nataly Kogan gives overworked, disaffected readers hope—and a roadmap for turning optimism into action."

ALEX SOOJUNG-KIM PANG, PHD   author of *Rest* and *Shorter*

"This book will help you make better choices about where to invest your energy and stop 'shoulding' yourself—at work and outside of work."

ALICIA DAVIS   director of Global Finance Learning and Development, Dell

THE

AWESOME

Break Free from Daily Burnout,

HUMAN

Struggle Less, and Thrive More

PROJECT

in Work and Life

NATALY KOGAN

sounds true

BOULDER, COLORADO

Sounds True
Boulder, CO 80306

Published 2022

Cover design by Jennifer Miles
Book design by Linsey Dodaro

The wood used to produce this book is from Forest
Stewardship Council (FSC) certified forests, recycled
materials, or controlled wood.

Printed in Canada

BK06211

Library of Congress Cataloging-in-Publication Data
Names: Kogan, Nataly, author.
Title: The awesome human project : how to break free from
daily burnout, struggle less, and thrive more in work and life /
by Nataly Kogan. Description: Boulder, CO : Sounds True, 2022.
| "Based on the science-backed Happier Method"--Title page.
Identifiers: LCCN 2021022119 (print) | LCCN 2021022120 (eb-
ook) | ISBN 9781683647850 (hardback) | ISBN 9781683647867
(ebook) Subjects: LCSH: Happiness. | Self-actualization
(Psychology) Classification: LCC BF575.H27 K63 2022 (print)
| LCC BF575.H27 (ebook) | DDC 158--dc23 LC record available
at https://lccn.loc.gov/2021022119 LC ebook record available at
https://lccn.loc.gov/2021022120

10 9 8 7 6 5 4 3 2 1

For my Mia (still).
I love you more,
always.

CONTENTS

The
Awesome
Human
Manifesto

You can't give what you don't have.

Taking care of your emotional, mental, and physical energy
is not a luxury but your responsibility to yourself,
your work, and the people you care about.

You can struggle less even when life is challenging.

You can struggle less through life's inevitable ups and downs
by creating a more supportive relationship with yourself,
your thoughts and emotions—and other people.

You are in charge of your emotional fitness.

Emotional fitness is a skill you can improve through practice
and it will help you struggle less and thrive more,
no matter where you begin.

You can talk back to your brain.

When your brain offers you unhelpful thoughts that
cause you to struggle, tap into your courage to talk
back to your brain and edit your thoughts.

Your humanness is what makes you awesome.

Give up trying to be tough or always positive and embrace
yourself fully, with all the mistakes and imperfections,
as you grow into the fullest expression of yourself.

Read This First:

My Dear Awesome Human Letter to You
(This is not a boring introduction, so don't go skipping it!)

Dear Awesome Human,

Did your brain just go: *What?! I am not awesome! I'm not good enough to be awesome; I haven't done enough to be called awesome!*

I get it. My brain used to do this a lot, too.

So I'm going to kindly but firmly talk back to your brain (you'll be learning to do this soon!):

Being an Awesome Human has absolutely nothing to do with being perfect or reaching some made-up "enough" accomplishment metric!

Awesome Humans don't seek perfection in themselves or their lives because they know it's not possible. They treat themselves with self-compassion and courageously talk back to their brain when it offers them thoughts that make them feel like crap or get in the way of doing stuff that matters. They boldly embrace the ups and downs of life and their own emotions, including the difficult ones. (You'll never see an Awesome Human trying to fake being tough or positive all the time.)

Awesome Humans are leaders—not because of their titles at work or even having a job but because they care about positively impacting other people's capacity to thrive. But they know that they can't give what they don't have, so they make fueling their emotional, mental, and physical energy their number one priority (and learn to quiet their brain's chatter when it calls this being selfish).

There is an Awesome Human within every single one of us. Yes, that means you, too! And I am so incredibly grateful that you've made the *courageous* choice to undertake your Awesome Human Project so you can embrace your inner Awesome Human, struggle less, and thrive more in every part of your life.

Let's go straight to the struggle part because it's at the core of my Bigger Why for writing this book:

Being human is hard. Life is full of challenges, changes, and uncertainty. Sometimes your days can feel like a game of Whack-a-Mole. You're just trying to get as much done as you can and run as fast as you can, and you can hardly keep up.

As if that weren't hard enough, your brain is telling you all kinds of stories that cause you to struggle more.

You know the stories I mean:

You're not good enough!

You're not getting enough done!

You should feel guilty for not working harder, not being a better parent, not remembering to call your friends and family on every birthday. And how dare you take a break when there is still dinner to cook, and you have ten more emails you need to send for work!

I didn't have to use my imagination for these stories. They are the ones my brain tells me often. And I spent most of my life believing them and taking them to heart. I showered myself with harsh criticism anytime I made a mistake or didn't live up to my impossibly high expectations. Every day felt like a race to accomplish more and to run away from the feelings of dread, stress, and utter overwhelm that hung over me.

But I was convinced this was the only way: to live a meaningful life and reach big, audacious goals, you *had* to struggle. So I did! I even prided myself on being able to tough it out without wasting time on silly things like self-care. That was for "the weak," and I was strong: a refugee; an entrepreneur; and a successful woman in the male-dominated industries of venture capital, consulting, and tech. As a leader and a mom, I adopted the martyr mentality and believed that as long as I cared about the emotional and mental well-being of others and sacrificed my own for them, I was doing it right.

Until one day, I couldn't run anymore. I'd completely burned out and had nothing left to give—not to my work, my family and friends, or myself. I didn't have an ounce more of emotional, mental, or physical energy to keep going. This was the scariest time of my life. It's not an exaggeration to say that I faced losing everything meaningful to me.

When I look back, I realize that I had been experiencing *daily burnout* for decades. Every day, I depleted my energy reservoir to almost empty. I rarely paused to fill it by taking a break, doing something that brought me joy, or even saying a kind word to myself. I didn't feel I deserved to do this or had time for it.

Worse, I didn't imagine there *could* be another way. I had become used to a certain degree of emotional pain and physical exhaustion, and that was my normal. Eventually, my daily burnout snowballed into an overwhelming burnout that I couldn't just grit my way through.

Of course, I wanted to feel better. But I had resigned myself to the story that struggle was inevitable. My struggle, my exhaustion, my endless harsh self-talk were badges of honor. They reminded me that, yes, I was living a meaningful life and achieving important things. I didn't have the courage to pause and look within myself. I didn't know how to recognize that I had a dysfunctional relationship with my brain, my emotions, and myself, and I had the power to change this dynamic.

You can change this dynamic within yourself. You CAN struggle less, even when life is difficult. My Bigger Why for writing this book is to help you do this and to share the life-changing lessons I learned as I found my way out of hopelessness and burnout.

The first one, and perhaps the most important, is this:

Challenges in life are constant. But struggle is optional.

You CAN reduce how much you struggle daily. The whole "Struggle is real!" thing? I'm calling its bluff.

Challenge is what happens on the outside. Struggle comes from the mindset with which you approach life's challenges; the way you treat yourself; and the relationship you have with your thoughts, emotions, and other people.

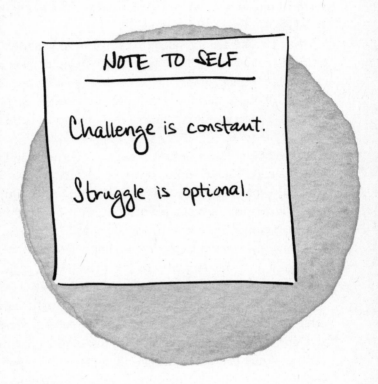

NOTE TO SELF

Challenge is constant.

Struggle is optional.

You will struggle more if you:

- never refuel your energy reservoir.

- choose to believe the negative and deflating stories your brain tells you.

- allow your brain's fear of danger to cloud your judgment and cause more stress.

- judge yourself for having certain emotions and try to have only positive feelings.

- try to do everything alone and hide your emotions from others.

You will struggle less when you:

- fuel your emotional, mental, and physical energy.

- treat yourself with compassion.

- recognize that you can talk back to your brain when it distorts reality and makes it harder to move forward.

- acknowledge and accept the many different emotions you feel, including the difficult ones.

- cultivate emotionally honest and meaningful relationships with other people.

When you struggle less, you have so much more energy and capacity to work through the challenges life and work bring your way. And you can find ways to grow and evolve through tough times, not just survive through them.

You embrace and unleash the Awesome Human within you.

Michelangelo talked about the sculpture already being inside a piece of marble and as a sculptor, his job was to chisel away the excess. During your Awesome Human Project, you will learn the skills to chisel away the obstacles so you can fully embrace the Awsome Human within you. In my not-humble opinion, this is the most important project of your life!

I'm so honored to lead you on this incredible journey.

So let's begin your Awesome Human Project!
With excitement and gratitude,

Nataly

P.S. My email is natalyk@happier.com, and if you have questions or want to share something with me as you do this book, I would LOVE to hear from you. I read all the emails myself, although it takes me a bit of time to get through them.

Your Awesome Human

Part I

Backstory

- Nataly's story
- Happier Method 101
- Your brain on challenge

Part II

Warm-up

- Develop your Awesome Human qualities

Project at a Glance

Part III

5-week challenge

- Learn and practice the

5 core

Emotional Fitness Skills

Part IV

Ongoing practice

- Quick tips for regular practice

- SOS: Help for when you are struggling

How to Do Your Awesome Human Project

A quick note about illustrations in your Awesome Human Project: I drew these myself! (And I wrote all of your Notes to Self, too, just like I write them for myself in my journal.) I had to give myself a bajillion pep talks to quiet my inner critic, who was yelling that I'm not a professional illustrator, asking what if the readers don't like them, and blah blah blah! I want you to know this so that (1) you can be kind in your judgment, and (2) you know I have to practice the same skills I'm sharing with you. (Yes! You will be learning how to quiet your inner critic in a little bit!)

- **Read the Back Story (part I, chapters 1-3).** Here I'll share a bit about what I discovered on my journey from success to burnout and learning how to live and work in a way that fuels me rather than drains me. I'll give you a quick overview of the Happier Method™ at the core of your Awesome Human Project. You'll also get a mini neuroscience lesson to understand how your brain reacts to challenges, and I promise it won't be boring.

- **Practice developing your Awesome Human Qualities (part II, chapters 4-8).** Think of this part of your project as warm-up before your emotional fitness training. Stretching before a workout improves body awareness and keeps your muscles loose so you have full range of motion as you exercise. Developing your Awesome Human Qualities will improve your emotional awareness and boost your courage and self-compassion, which you'll need to successfully practice your emotional fitness skills.

- **Do the Five-Week Emotional Fitness Challenge (part III, chapters 9-13).** If you can, I would love for you to focus on one emotional fitness skill per week for five weeks. But don't stress if life makes this difficult to do. Adjust this part of your project to work for you. (When you get to this part, I'll share some suggestions for how to adjust the weeks if you need to.)

- **Integrate the skills into your daily life (part IV, chapters 14-15).** In the final part of the book, I share my favorite practices and tips to help you create an ongoing emotional fitness practice.

- **I want you to DO this book, not just read this book!** The only way to develop your Awesome Human Qualities and emotional fitness skills is by DOING the practices in each chapter. They aren't complicated and don't take a lot of time, I promise. But you gotta practice. (Fair warning: You will get sick of me saying "practice," and I'm totally okay with that!)

- **SOS: For those times when you're struggling**. I created a special section at the end of the book with Notes to Self and page numbers for where to go in the book for specific advice and practices to help you get out of the Valley of Struggle.

Awesome Human Awards

Now is a great time to tell you that you'll be getting awards as you go through your Awesome Human Project! Yessss!

I think it sucks that we get tons of awards as kids and then almost none when we grow up. I want to change that! You will have an opportunity to give yourself Awesome Human Awards after you practice your Awesome Human Qualities and emotional fitness skills. Because I can't be there to check on you, we'll use the honor system: When you feel you've earned it, you get it. Be honestly generous with your Awesome Human Awards!

Speaking of being there, I wish I could jump through time and space and encourage, support, and cheer for you in person as you do your Awesome Human Project! But I can't, which might be lucky for you because I can get pretty loud. So I've done the next best thing: I've recorded some video pep talks so you can fuel up when you need a boost. You can find them on my website, natalykogan.com, in the Awesome Human Project section.

Oh, and when you go to my website, there might or might not be some other Awesome Human surprises there. (Of course, they will be there; I love surprises!)

Okay, are you ready?

Let's go!

PART I

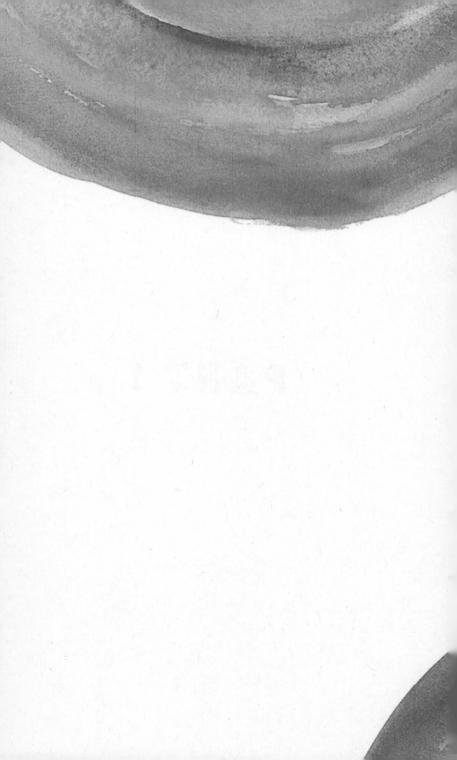

THE BACK STORY

The Teacher and the **Method** at the **Core** of Your **Awesome Human Project**

CHAPTER 1

My Story

Hi, I'm Nataly, and for most of my life, struggle was my religion.

Yes, you read that right. I'm proud to be introduced at conferences as one of the leading experts on emotional fitness. I've successfully taught the skills in this book to tens of thousands of people, teams, and leaders. Yet I used to completely ignore my mental health and emotional fitness. I believed that doing anything meaningful in life had to involve struggle.

Got something done at work? My brain would tell me how I should have done it faster and better and, oh, how I didn't get nearly enough done.

Played with my daughter? My brain was ready with how I wasn't focused on her enough or spending enough time with her and how guilty I should feel for not balancing work and family.

The hotel gave us the wrong room? My brain had me spinning into a full-on stress cyclone in seconds: *This always happens to me; no one knows how to do their jobs well; this whole vacation is ruined! Wait, can I blame my husband for this?*

It was exhausting to live this way, but my only response was to work harder, do more, and try to achieve my way out of the struggle somehow. It was what I knew. Coming to the United States with my parents as refugees from Russia when I was thirteen years old taught me that anything worthwhile was on the other side of struggle—achievement, fulfillment, happiness, success, becoming a US citizen, being a good human being.

I was a teenager who didn't speak English and didn't have a clue about how to navigate school. My parents couldn't offer any guidance. I felt lost, and I hung on to the only thing I knew how to do: work really, really hard. And working really hard helped! I learned to speak English without an accent, graduated with every conceivable honor from Wesleyan University, had a series of high-level, impressive jobs at companies like McKinsey and Microsoft, and became a managing director in a venture capital firm at the age of twenty-six (an industry with less than 6 percent women). I also started and was part of the senior team at five startups, some more successful than others.

I did all of this by the time I was thirty-five years old.

Somewhere in there I also married Avi, my college sweetheart, and we had a beautiful daughter, Mia. I loved being able to take care of my family in all ways, including financially, because I was the majority breadwinner for many years.

But all of this success and chronic overachievement came at a huge cost and always with struggle.

I was overwhelmed and exhausted all the time, denying myself most emotional and physical nourishment, like sleep or even rest. My mind kept a running list of all the mistakes I was making as a leader, mom, daughter, wife, friend—and I berated myself nonstop. My inner critic was in constant overdrive. Many days I had a heavy sense of dread—an ominous feeling that I was on the edge of burnout—but I didn't know how to change. Although there were many wonderful moments, comforts, and people in my life, I was so disconnected from my daily experience and *my own feelings* that I wasn't actually enjoying very many of them.

Somehow, the idea of investing time or energy in my own well-being felt indulgent, weak, and frankly like a waste of time. Phrases like *self-care* made me cringe! I wore my exhaustion and stress like badges of honor.

NOTE TO SELF

Exhaustion
is not
a badge of honor.

The fact was, I had no role models for what success without this level of self-sacrifice looked like. I wasn't reading in the press about leaders taking breaks at work or practicing self-care and self-compassion. Instead, I was reading about Tesla CEO Elon Musk, who slept four hours a night and ran five companies while sending emails from his kids' soccer games, and Marissa Mayer, then CEO of Yahoo, who put a nursery next to her office so she could work longer hours without having to go home to see her daughter.

It always felt like I was expected to change into my work identity and check all that touchy-feely emotional stuff at the door. I did it gladly because I had no idea how to deal with my emotions anyway.

Yet I felt terrible. I remember one morning feeling like my body weighed a thousand pounds, and I could hardly move. I felt that way for a week, still trying to stick to my normal routine of work, taking care of my daughter, and going to the gym, until one day I literally couldn't lift a two-pound weight. My friend, a physician, encouraged me to make an appointment with a functional medicine doctor. I had no idea what that meant, but I did it, reluctantly.

The doctor I went to see asked me a bunch of questions, mostly about my lifestyle, my work habits, how much I slept, and what I did to refuel myself. I'd hoped he would just take some blood samples and tell me I had a weird infection easily cured with antibiotics. He didn't. After about twenty minutes, he paused and told me that he knew what was wrong with me. He said that he had many patients like me: people who work nonstop, treat themselves like a machine they expect to operate 24/7, and achieve a lot of success doing that for a time. But then they find that their ability to get work done begins to deteriorate, their deals aren't going the way they want, and they start having problems at work and at home. Around forty years old, if they don't change their lifestyle and make their emotional and mental health a priority, they burn out. He was convinced this was the path I was on unless I was willing to make some changes in my lifestyle.

I was thirty-four at the time. As the doctor talked, I remember thinking I would never be one of *those* people, whose work suffered or who burned out. They were weak! I was a force of nature.

Oh, how great our minds can be at creating an alternate reality! By this point, I already had a hard time making clear decisions at work and remember being surprised at how often I would get completely stuck in a spin cycle of conflicting thoughts. I'd started to lack confidence during presentations—to investors, partners, my team—which felt disheartening because I've always been comfortable with public speaking. I had fewer and fewer days when I felt anywhere near on top of things or that I was doing a good job.

My capacity to work was suffering in every way, as was my ability to function at home. I was going through the motions as best I could but feeling more and more disconnected from my husband and daughter. I hated waking up in the morning to face another day. Yet I refused to pause long enough to be honest with myself. **I didn't have the courage to look within myself or to even consider that there could be another way to live and work.**

So, I dismissed the doctor's words, even though he did a bunch of tests and found that I had severe adrenal deficiency caused by chronic stress. Because I was so exhausted, I had no choice but to get more sleep than my usual four to five hours a night for the next few weeks, which helped the worst symptoms subside. I was in the clear, I proudly thought. The doom-and-gloom scenario the doctor had talked about was for people who clearly weren't as tough as I was. The doctor was wrong about me.

And I was right: He *was* wrong about me. My burnout came at thirty-eight, not forty. I overachieved in that, too.

It took being at risk of losing everything meaningful to me—including my company, my team, my marriage, and my family—to hear the wake-up call.

As painful as it was to admit this to myself, it turned out that the very things I'd always rejected as having nothing to do with my ability to be a great leader, entrepreneur, mom, wife, and human were essential to it: things like learning how to rest before I became exhausted, reacting to mistakes with self-compassion rather than harshness, embracing challenging emotions rather than stuffing them down, and recognizing that sometimes things were outside my control and I could choose not to waste my energy flipping out about how they "should be." (For the record: this is all still a work in progress and part of my Awesome Human Project, just as it will be part of yours.)

But it's not like I realized all this overnight. No way! Even as I was losing my grip on everything in my life, I was resisting making any changes. **I'd gotten used to living with a high degree of emotional pain and convinced myself that I could just keep going the way I was.**

There's a parallel between chronic emotional pain and chronic physical pain. About ten years ago, I started to feel a sharp, shooting pain in both of my heels. It would come and go, and it wasn't terrible, so I just ignored it.

The sharp, shooting pain got worse and worse, especially because I take a five-mile walk every day. There were mornings when I got out of bed and shrieked and thought I would faint. I'd diagnosed myself with plantar fasciitis (thanks, Google!), but I figured somehow it would just go away.

And then one day, the pain was so bad that I cried. I couldn't walk, and it wouldn't go away even when I didn't put any pressure on my feet. I couldn't play with my daughter, go to work, or stand in the kitchen to make dinner. My husband finally convinced me to go to a doctor, who was surprised when I told him that I'd had severe pain for years.

I remember what I said: "I'm used to pain, so I just got used to it. Also, I'm really busy, so I just didn't have the time."

If you want to call me nuts for saying I was too busy to do something about such intense pain, go ahead, but sadly, I'm not unique. I had been experiencing daily burnout for years, and even though I felt the emotional strain of it, I refused to do anything about it until one day the pain became so unbearable, I was forced to confront it.

There's a reason courage is one of the five Awesome Human Qualities you'll be developing: making the choice to look within myself and change my relationship with my thoughts and my emotions was one of the hardest things I've ever done.

I had to drop the story I'd made up about who I was: a hard-working force of nature, an overachiever who was meant to always struggle and could tolerate the emotional pain a meaningful life required. Our stories become our shields, so putting them down requires courage.

It was also hard because I had no idea what to do next. Making the choice to reduce struggle and improve your emotional fitness is a huge step, but it doesn't show you the path. So I read books and research from every discipline you can imagine—including psychology, neuroscience, spirituality, and behavioral economics—and created exercises to put what I learned into practice. I began to work with a woman who became my spiritual teacher, even though just a few months earlier I'd rejected spirituality as "that thing people who can't hack it in real life resort to."

It took time, courage, and more supportive self-talk than I'd ever heard from myself in my entire life, but slowly, I was climbing out of the darkness. The process was messy, sometimes painful, sometimes joyful, and often sideways before I felt I was moving forward. But the more I practiced, the more courage I felt to keep going, to embrace my inner Awesome Human fully and with care.

I used the method I'm going to teach you, the Happier Method™, to climb out of the darkest, most hopeless place I've ever been onto a path where I experience less struggle in my daily experience. Also, my capacity to positively impact other people has expanded in ways I could never have imagined.

I always thought that to focus on my emotional well-being, I'd have to trade off achievement, success, getting stuff done, and taking care of other people. I couldn't have been

NOTE TO SELF

You don't need to choose between emotional well-being and success.

more wrong. Improving my emotional fitness has made me better in every way—as a creator, author, entrepreneur, speaker, leader, mom, wife, friend, daughter, and human. I can't tell you how amazing it feels to be a light in the lives of others rather than heavy energy, which is what I used to bring so often to the people I loved the most.

I wrote this book to help you reduce struggle and emotional pain *before* they become unbearable and you burn out. I want to catch you before you fall and teach you the mindset shifts, skills, and practices to strengthen your emotional fitness so you can struggle less and live with more meaning, ease, and joy. I want to help you use these skills to embrace your inner Awesome Human. And if you are in that dark place or stuck in a cycle of daily burnout, I promise you that doing this project can help you find your way out of it.

This is my commitment to you.

CHAPTER 2

The (Updated!) Happier Method™

Now that you know a bit about me and why I am so passionate about sharing with you what I've learned, I want to give you a super-quick overview of the Happier Method™, which is at the foundation of your Awesome Human Project. I created this method to help myself heal from my burnout, although at the time, I had no idea I was creating a method, much less that I would eventually teach it to tens of thousands of people. But I'm so grateful that what I learned from my own challenges—and a lot of research—can help so many others, including you!

The Happier Method™ is based on three core principles:

1. Challenge is constant. Struggle is optional.

Big or small, challenges are an inevitable part of life. Although you can't control what or when challenges come your way, you can learn to struggle less through them. And when you struggle less, you have more energy, clarity, and capacity to work through them, help other people, and not just survive but thrive. Yep, even when times are really difficult!

How do you struggle less? By creating a more supportive relationship with yourself, your thoughts and emotions, and other people (a.k.a. strengthening your emotional fitness), which brings me to the second principle of the Happier Method™.

2. Emotional fitness is a SKILL you can improve through practice.

Emotional fitness is not something lucky people have and unlucky ones don't. It's not a quality bestowed on us by our genes or life circumstances.

It's a skill you can develop, cultivate, and improve.

Just as you can develop your physical fitness, you can develop your emotional fitness. But instead of your body, you're training your brain—to help you navigate the roller coaster of life instead of causing you to struggle with all kinds of unhelpful thoughts.

And just so we're clear from the start: Improving your emotional fitness is not about becoming tough or never having difficult feelings! Trying to "always be positive" only increases stress and anxiety. A key emotional fitness skill you'll be mastering during your Awesome Human Project is learning how to embrace the full range of human emotions, including the difficult and uncomfortable ones, and support yourself to work through them with less struggle.

3. Small changes = big impact.

You don't need to make dramatic life changes to struggle less and thrive more. You don't need to put that kind of pressure on yourself because overcommitting only sets you up for failure. When we're tired or stressed, our brain simply can't give us the discipline to make huge changes.

Small shifts in mindset and in how you respond to your brain's thoughts and emotions—including during your interactions with other people—can make a huge difference.

> **NOTE TO SELF**
>
> You don't need to make dramatic life changes to struggle less and thrive more.

Every single moment, you have a choice to make small inner shifts to help yourself struggle less, even when you're going through a difficult time or facing a tough challenge. The important thing is to make the choice to do it.

You can do it, and it will make a difference, I promise you.

Here are the five core emotional fitness skills you'll be learning and practicing during your Awesome Human Project:

1. **Acceptance**: Acknowledging your feelings and the situation with clarity instead of getting caught up in your brain's stories and using that as your starting point for moving forward.

2. **Gratitude**: Making an active choice to appreciate the small, positive moments in everyday life—even when times are challenging—and sharing your appreciation for other people with them.

3. **Self-Care**: Intentionally fueling your emotional, mental, and physical energy.

4. **Intentional Kindness**: Being actively kind and compassionate toward others without expecting anything in return.

5. **The Bigger Why**: Regularly connecting with your sense of meaning and purpose by identifying how your daily activities and tasks support bigger goals, help others, or contribute to a cause you believe in.

I'm certain that none of these words is new to you—this isn't rocket science.

Although I promise that you'll gain a new and fresh perspective on each one, the most important thing you'll learn is how to *practice them as skills*, intentionally and consistently, and how to use them to train your brain to cause you less struggle so you can embrace your inner Awesome Human and thrive!

A note on thriving:

I love the word *thrive*. To thrive means to flourish and grow vigorously. I believe this is what we're here to do, in this complex and beautiful life of ours. And it means something different to each of us, which I also love—there is no prescription for what thriving looks like, but you definitely know it when you experience it.

Wherever you are right now, I'm confident it is possible for you to thrive more.

Even if you're feeling low, overwhelmed, or perhaps even in the dark place where I found myself several years ago, when you commit to practicing your emotional fitness skills, you can learn to struggle less. Your wins might feel small at first. In the journal I kept during my first year of healing from burnout, I wrote that I had an hour where I felt I wasn't fighting with myself or my reality, and that felt amazing! So, you might begin with an hour, which will lead to days, which will lead to more.

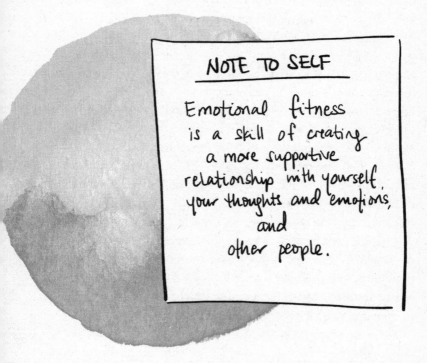

NOTE TO SELF

Emotional fitness is a skill of creating a more supportive relationship with yourself, your thoughts and emotions, and other people.

On the flip side, if you've been practicing some of these skills and have a more cooperative relationship with your brain, I am confident that diving in deeper will help to unleash within you a greater capacity to thrive and help others around you.

I want to give a special shoutout to you if you've read my previous book, *Happier Now*.

"Hi!!!!!!!!" (You gotta imagine me, running toward you with confetti coming out of my ears, holding a huge bunch of bright yellow balloons, when you read this!)

Thank you for coming back for more! I recognize that some of the skills I share in this book might be familiar. Awesome! It takes seven repetitions before we truly understand an idea, so unless you read *Happier Now* seven times, I promise you won't be bored, and the refreshers will be useful. (If you *have* read *Happier Now* seven times, I would really love to say thank you—my email is natalyk@happier.com!)

The Awesome Human Project builds on the foundation you learned in *Happier Now*: I've significantly expanded the Happier Method™ and have added tons of new practices, mindset shifts, concepts, Talk Back to Your Brain scripts, and more. I wrote *Happier Now* as I was still finding my way to living with less struggle, and I hadn't yet fully grasped all of the shifts I had made and the powerful impact they had. I was too close to it all and needed time to reflect before being able to put it into words, which I'm doing with immense excitement in *The Awesome Human Project*.

Something else became part of my Bigger Why for writing this book: I kept hearing from *Happier Now* readers who told me that they'd owned the book for months or years before they found the courage to actually open it and read it. Some shared that they were struggling so much, it was too difficult to even think about becoming happier.

So I wanted to go straight to the struggle because that is actually where I began myself. My life didn't become less challenging after I began to develop and practice the qualities and skills I'm sharing with you in this book. But I became more emotionally fit and developed a more supportive relationship with myself, my thoughts, and my emotions, and that helped me struggle *less* through those challenges. And when I struggled less, I had more energy, felt happier, and had so much more to give to my work and the people I love.

This is what you will learn how to do during your Awesome Human Project, and it's the raison d'être for this book!

CHAPTER 3

Meet Your Brain on Challenge
(a.k.a. a Mini Neuroscience Lesson)

Imagine this scenario, which you've probably experienced more than once: the Tense Boss.

You've got a meeting with your boss, in person or maybe virtually by video. As the meeting begins, you notice that your boss isn't smiling like she normally does and seems tense.

What is your reaction?

If you're like most people I know, your brain says something like: *Oh, crap, she is upset with me; I did something wrong; she hated that email I sent. I totally screwed up; I knew it. She hates my work. I think I'm about to get fired. Yep, definitely. Is our whole team getting fired? OMG!*

All these thoughts cause you to tense up—obviously. You aren't even paying attention to what your boss is saying. In fact, you're so distracted that you're stumbling through the conversation, and your boss gets frustrated.

You notice this and take it as confirmation that she is extremely upset and definitely considering firing you. As you leave your meeting, you're freaking out. You text a colleague to say that you're probably getting fired, which causes your colleague to freak out and think maybe he is next.

You spend the rest of your workday in full-on stress overwhelm mode, getting very little work done. By now you've confirmed to yourself that you definitely suck at your job, so it's no surprise that your boss is thinking of firing you. When you see an email from her in your inbox at the end of the day, you close your laptop without even opening the email. You know what it says.

Okay, stop. Cut!

Phew, catch your breath for a bit—that was stressful! Even writing this scenario was stressful because I was reliving similar meetings I'd had. The Tense Boss scenario is a great way for me to introduce you to your brain on challenge. Understanding how your brain reacts to challenges and stressful situations—a.k.a. life—is so powerful. Once you have the awareness of why your brain is doing what it's doing, you can make the choice to shift your thoughts so that they help you get through this challenging situation with less struggle, stress, and anxiety.

When I began to read neuroscience and psychology research to try to find a way out of my burnout, it felt like shining a light into a dark room. Even before I did a single thing to change, I felt a sense of relief.

I wasn't failing at life because I felt overwhelmed and burned out! Instead, I had let my brain run the show on autopilot. I believed every story it told me about myself, other people, different situations, and my life without ever pausing to ask if these stories were true or helpful. I knew I'd have to develop a completely different relationship with my brain in order to live with less struggle, but this awareness on its own was huge. (It still is!)

So, strap in for a little amateur neuroscience lesson!

Bad news first:

Your brain doesn't care about your feelings. It doesn't care if you feel happy, sad, confident, or doubtful. It definitely isn't concerned with your level of emotional fitness.

Before you get angry at your brain, here's the good news:

Your brain's main job is to keep you safe from danger. This is really good news because staying alive is awesome.

Your brain takes its main responsibility of keeping you safe very seriously. Although these days we rarely face physical danger (say, a pack of wolves running at us), the brain has adapted to look for symbolic or psychological danger (like your boss seeming tense). Your brain is always looking for danger but especially when you're dealing with challenging, unfamiliar, or uncertain situations. Familiarity signals safety; anything new or uncertain signals possible danger.

Because danger usually comes with a lot of negative stimuli, your brain has become really good at looking for, noticing, and remembering them. Whether it's a pack of wolves or your tense boss, in both scenarios your brain notices these signs of danger immediately. To totally geek out on this—which, I must warn you, I love to do—two-thirds of the neurons in your amygdala, the part of your brain that controls your emotional responses, are dedicated to detecting negative stimuli. (After your brain detects negative stimuli—a.k.a. possible danger!—it activates a stress response you probably know as "fight or flight.")

Let me introduce you to your brain's negativity bias.

Your brain's tendency to more readily register anything negative that could signify danger is called a negativity bias. We all have it: all of our brains are more sensitive to noticing anything negative than anything positive.

The brain is also much better at remembering negative stimuli because they might signal danger in the future. If you see a pack of wolves once, you'll run faster next time. Very useful.

But the brain's tendency to remember bad stuff better than good stuff can also cause you unnecessary emotional pain. Let's say you deliver a presentation at work. A few of your colleagues tell you what a great job you did, but one makes a negative comment. What are you thinking about for the rest of the day—the positive feedback or the negative comment?

Your brain's negativity bias has the answer: You're way more likely to obsess about the critical comment than to think about all the positive words your colleagues shared. (I'm all for taking constructive feedback, by the way. The part where your brain wastes your energy and deflates your confidence endlessly ruminating on any negative comments is where I have a problem.)

The way your brain sees it, the cost of missing negative stimuli and potentially putting you in danger is much greater than not noticing something that makes you feel good.

Keeping you alive is great and all, but your brain's negativity bias means you don't actually see your reality accurately; the negative stuff is exaggerated. Focusing only on what could potentially go wrong increases your stress, anxiety, and worry. The negativity bias is one way your brain causes you to struggle, and you'll learn how to correct it using the skill of Gratitude.

Think back to the Tense Boss scenario. Your brain immediately zeroed in on what was negative—your boss wasn't smiling and seemed tense—which it took as a sign of danger. You felt stressed, and your brain began to create negative stories about why she was acting that way and what might happen.

But wait: Why did your brain jump so quickly from "My boss is not smiling and seems tense" to "She must think I'm doing a bad job, and I'm getting fired!" Where did that come from?

To answer this question, you need to understand your brain's least favorite thing in the world: uncertainty.

Your brain hates uncertainty!

Uncertainty makes it much more difficult for your brain to keep you safe from danger. By definition, uncertainty means that your brain can't tell what's safe and what isn't. Think about how stressful it is to be in any kind of limbo. In fact, researchers have found that our brains would rather know *for sure* that something terrible is going to happen than face uncertainty.

Your brain does something else when it's faced with uncertainty: It tries to create certainty by making up stories. And because of its negativity bias, the stories it makes up are often negative and somewhat dramatic. That's how "My boss is not smiling and seems tense" turns into "My boss hates my work and is going to fire me!"

By the way, our brains loooove stories! When we hear or tell a story, the pleasure centers in our brains light up. And this is true even if the story is a scary one. Stories give our brains a sense of control of our reality. The brain loves to feel in control, which brings us to the third way your brain causes you unnecessary stress and anxiety:

Your brain loves to jump to conclusions.

Our brains rely on patterns to help them recognize things quickly, without having to learn about each object and situation from scratch every time we encounter it. When danger appears, your brain wants to be able to notice it immediately.

The first time you see a pack of wolves in the distance, your brain has to study it pretty carefully to understand what's going on. It looks at the shapes, listens to the noises, and analyzes the speed with which the shapes are moving toward you to determine your next best step (RUN!). But the next time you see a pack of wolves, your brain doesn't need to study the details. When it sees an outline of the pack in the distance, it'll tell you to RUN!

But the brain's tendency to jump to conclusions can create danger when there isn't any. Maybe in the past, when your boss was unhappy with your work, she didn't smile and looked tense, so your brain relied on something you experienced before. You had no evidence to support this conclusion, but you felt the stress anyway.

We don't see things as they are. We see them as we *believe* they are.

Of course, there could've been many other reasons for your boss's tenseness, but your brain didn't pause to think through them. When we are stressed out, our ability to consider different perspectives is compromised. Research shows we don't take the time to think through other points of view or listen when others contribute them. The brain considers all this analyzing wasted energy in the face of danger.

Just as your brain defaults to familiar patterns when it senses danger, it creates and defaults to patterns of belief about you. Many of these patterns come from your childhood. For example, if your parents always scolded you for not getting perfect grades, you might grow up to be a perfectionist who sets super-high standards, and you are only satisfied when you reach them. If your parents encouraged you not to get down on yourself for a low grade and simply focus on learning what you did wrong, you're less likely to expect perfection from yourself.

But don't blame your parents for all of your brain's unhelpful and negative thought patterns. Your brain creates many of these irrational beliefs—cognitive distortions, as psychologists call them—as you go through life. At their core, many cognitive distortions come from your brain's overzealous tendency to look for danger and to be overly sensitive to any possible sign of it (real or imagined).

I recognize that you might be tempted to get really annoyed at your brain right about now. Please don't. It's just trying to keep you safe and alive. But there is one thing you do need to do: you need to recognize that you are not at the mercy of your brain but in charge of it.

Say what?

It's easy to think your brain is in charge. After all, there is nothing we can do as human beings without our brains telling some part of our bodies to do it.

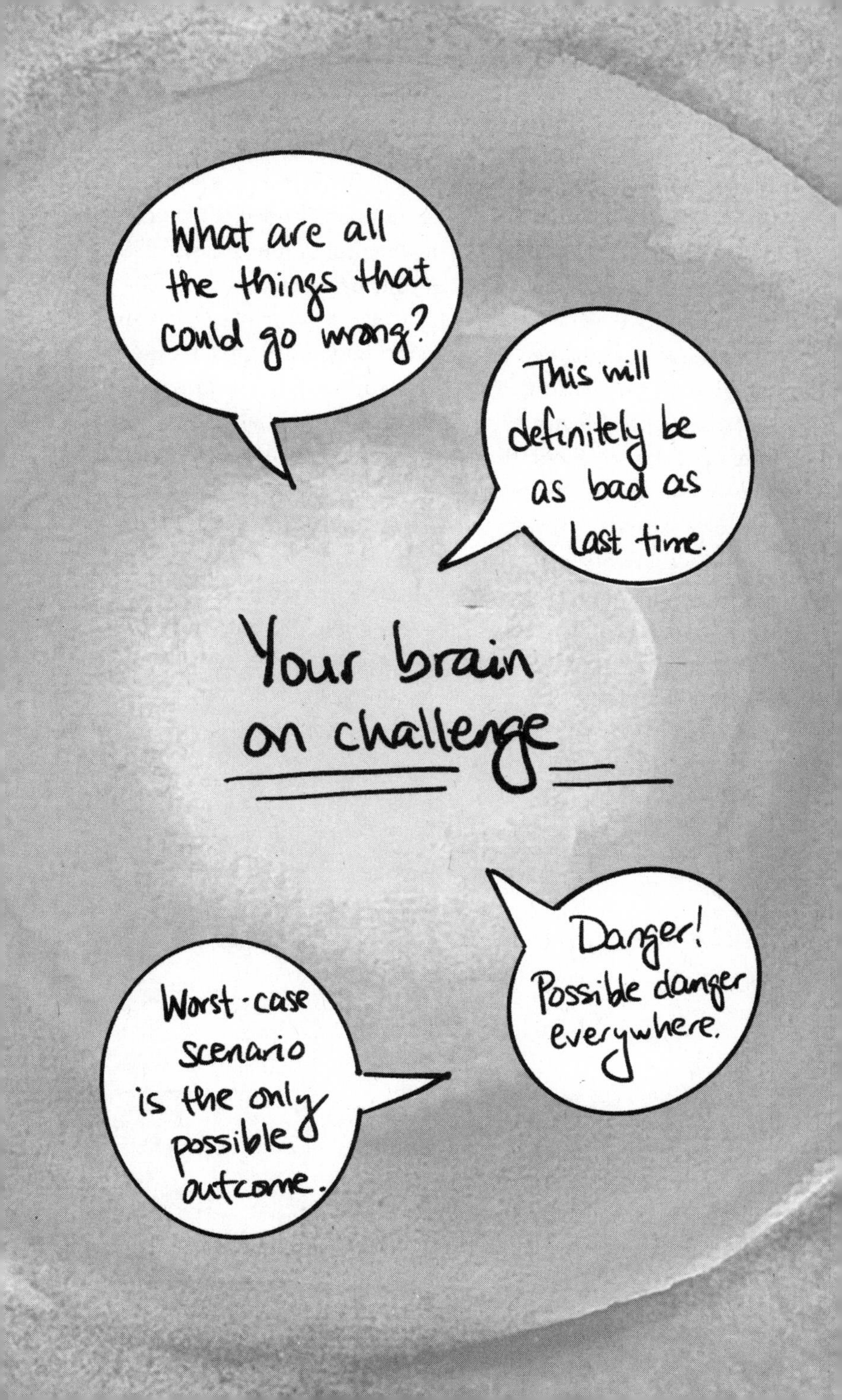

What are all the things that could go wrong?
This will definitely be as bad as last time.
Your brain on challenge
Danger! Possible danger everywhere.
Worst-case scenario is the only possible outcome.

But when it comes to your thoughts, you get to take the wheel, if you choose. Just because your brain offers you a thought doesn't mean you need to believe it and act upon it. You can question it, shift it so that it's more helpful to you, or discard it.

You can become the editor of your thoughts.

In cognitive behavioral therapy (CBT), of which I've been an amateur but dedicated student for many years, this is called cognitive restructuring. CBT is based on one core principle: our thoughts affect how we feel, so we can change how we feel by changing our thoughts. As you work through your Awesome Human Project, you will learn how to recognize when your brain is offering you distorted, incorrect, or un-helpful thoughts and how to edit them to reduce struggle.

Begin right now by practicing Struggle Awareness. Awareness is powerful. Once you become aware of thoughts that cause you to stress or struggle, you have a choice of what to do, and you can choose to shift them to be more helpful to you.

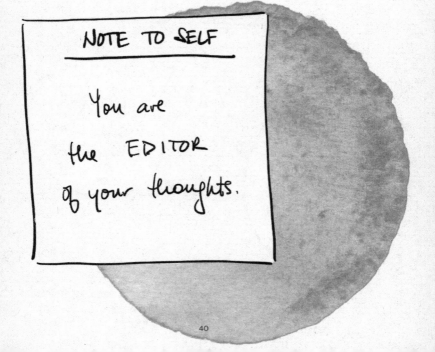

NOTE TO SELF

You are
the EDITOR
of your thoughts.

PRACTICE

Struggle Awareness

When you notice you are struggling with a challenge, difficulty, or frustration, ask yourself:

How is the way I'm thinking about this challenge or difficulty causing me to struggle more?

How might my brain's negativity bias be affecting my view of the situation?

Is my brain creating dramatic stories that aren't rooted in reality?

How are my brain's patterns of thinking affecting my ability to see this situation as it is versus how I assume it is based on my past experiences?

It can be helpful to put your thoughts in writing so you're better able to witness them.

Here are some examples of how you might shift your thoughts by using this practice:

More Struggle	Less Struggle
"Nothing ever works out for me like it does for other people."	"I've been through a lot of challenges, and things didn't always work out like I wish they had. But it doesn't mean things won't work out in the future."

"My friend hasn't texted me in a week, so she is definitely angry at me for something I did or said."

"I haven't heard from my friend in a while. I wonder if she is okay. I'll reach out."

"I always mess up during presentations because I'm so nervous, so I'm definitely going to bomb this one."

"This is an important presentation, so understandably I'm nervous, but I've practiced and even if I mess up a few times, it won't take away from the overall presentation."

"My boss wasn't smiling and seemed tense during our meeting, so she's definitely unhappy with me and my work and is probably going to fire me."

"My boss seems more tense than usual and I'm not sure why. I'll ask her how she is doing."

AWESOME HUMAN AWARD

After you've practiced Struggle Awareness a few times, proudly give yourself the **Brain Editor-in-Training** award! You're on your way to mastering this essential skill, and I hope you recognize just what a huge step you've taken in doing it.

PART II

THE WARM-UP

Developing Your **Awesome Human Qualities**

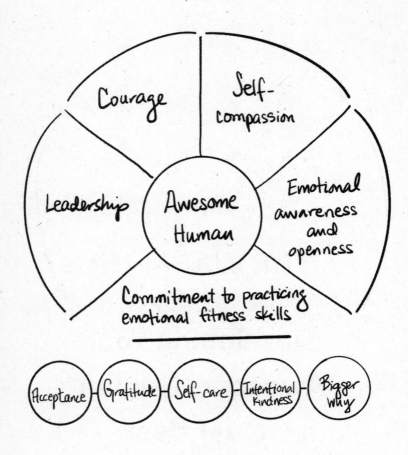

During part II of your Awesome Human Project, you're going to learn and develop the qualities it takes to be an Awesome Human. Then, in part III, you'll undertake a five-week challenge to strengthen your emotional fitness skills. Developing these qualities and skills is what allows you to embrace your Awesome Human.

Are you ready? You totally are—let's go!

CHAPTER 4

The Courage to Talk Back to Your Brain

Awesome Human Quality: Courage

In order to embrace your Awesome Human, you need courage. And it begins with having the courage to recognize that you're not powerless amid life's many challenges and you can *choose* to struggle less through them.

This is not an easy choice to make, and I resisted making it for·a very long time. So I know how far your brain will go to convince you that there isn't a choice, or even if you make it, it won't work. Your brain loves familiarity and predictability because they signal safety. So when you make the choice to change, to do something differently from how you've always done it, your brain will resist you with all its might.

This is why you need courage to talk back to your brain.

I'm going to ask you to dive right into the deep end with your courage and use it to make some cracks in the story of how "you've always been" and "how you are now." This won't be easy to do. We find comfort in the stories we come to believe about ourselves, and they become shields that prevent us from doing the inner work to struggle less and embrace our Awesome Human. If you stick to the story "this is just how I am," then you don't need to do anything to change. According to your story, you *can't* change; it's just how you are!

This was me for most of my life.

NOTE TO SELF

When your brain
tells you stories
that make you struggle

TALK BACK
To Your BRAIN!

I bought into the story that I was a superwoman and a force of nature who could do more in a day than most people, and I didn't need to do silly things like rest or be kind to myself. As a Russian Jewish refugee, I came from a lineage of suffering, so of course I was meant to fight the world, always have it tough, and struggle to achieve anything meaningful. Oh, and look, the women closest to me, my mom and her mom, always criticize themselves, never take time to rest or relax, and always find ways something could be made better or more perfect, so no wonder I'm this way!

My story was a convenient excuse to keep living on the edge of burnout for decades and avoid doing anything to change. I was afraid to let go of it, even after I had burned out, because I had no idea who I was if I wasn't a tough cookie and a force of nature, always fighting against the odds, doing the impossible, and working harder than anyone else.

We all have stories we believe about ourselves, and other people, the media, and our experiences definitely contribute to them. To be fair, not all of these stories are terrible. My stories that I'm always up for learning anything new, or I'm a super-creative person who finds ways to make ordinary experiences a little more special, are awesome! Thinking of myself that way gives me energy and fuel to learn new things and explore my creativity.

But many of our stories deflate and limit us, cause us to feel like we're not this or that enough, drain our emotional and mental energy, and drive us to burn out daily. These are the stories I want you to bust through with your courage.

What are the stories that cause you to struggle and get in your way?

I asked this question during one of my weekly Awesome Human Hour live sessions recently, and here are just a few stories people shared:

> I have to always be positive or I will bring other
> people down.

> I have to be helpful or people won't like me.

> I am a failure because I haven't achieved amazing things
> like curing cancer, solving world hunger, or running
> a company.

Bad things can happen to me if I don't worry
or try enough.

I can't do anything well, and the more I try, the more it
gets screwed up.

Are you nodding as you read through these? I was; I could relate to so many. But what struck me as I read them was how clear it was to me, as an outsider, that these stories couldn't possibly be completely accurate. It's difficult to recognize that about our own stories because we become so attached to them that we lose our objectivity.

The thing about stories is that they become self-fulfilling prophecies because of our brains' confirmation bias: the tendency to interpret information in a way that supports our existing beliefs and ignore information that goes counter to them. (This is another flavor of the brain's inclination to default to familiar thinking patterns.)

I recently interviewed Chris Brock, an author and podcast host from the United Kingdom, and he told me about a story that kept him trapped for many years:

"I was that guy who was picked last for every team at school, so I just figured, okay, I'm an underachiever, that's how my life is going to be," he said. Being an underachiever became his story, and his brain used it as a shield to prevent him from trying new things and taking on challenges. What's more, it interpreted Chris's actions, like not taking risks or applying for challenging jobs, as confirmation of him being an underachiever.

It's not easy to break free from the stories that cause you to struggle, but it is possible. And doing so requires the courageous decision to change your patterns of thinking by becoming the editor of your thoughts.

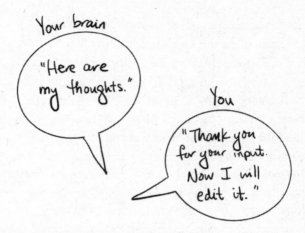

How to Edit Your Thoughts

As you learn to edit your thoughts so that they serve you rather than get in your way, here are two questions you need to ask yourself:

1. *Is this story true?* A good editor would never publish something not supported by the facts.

2. *Is this story helpful?* A great editor always thinks about how every story contributes to the over-all narrative, so ask yourself whether this story helps you to create a narrative of your life that you would like to see unfold. Does it help you thrive? Achieve goals meaningful to you? Show up the way you want for the people you care about?

In my case, my brain constantly looked for confirmation that, yep, I had to struggle and do everything on my own because I was a superwoman and could do it all and without help! But this story wasn't true! I was exhausted and burning out daily, evidence enough that I wasn't a superhuman but a regular human who needed rest and self-care. Many loving and caring people supported me, and so much of what I'd achieved was in part because of their help and encouragement.

Was Chris's story that he was an underachiever true? No! Chris told me that when a great job opportunity came up in New York City, he decided to take it and move there from England, without having a place to live or making other plans. It was a huge risk, and it was scary, but he jumped in and figured it out. Had he been honest about it, he would have seen how this experience pierced many holes in his story of being an underachiever.

Not only was my story of being a superwoman who had to struggle through life on her own untrue but also it was entirely unhelpful. It kept me trapped in a cycle of daily burnout and zapped my energy so I had less of it to work toward all the things I wanted to achieve. I also had less positive energy to share with the people I loved, and they often got the exhausted, overwhelmed, snapping-at-them Nataly.

It's impossible to know, but I'd like to think that had I paused to edit my story, I would have recognized that it wasn't true or helpful and given myself permission to take off my superwoman cape; respect my physical, mental, and emotional needs; and learn to ask for help when I needed it. Without a doubt, this would have saved me from so much struggle and perhaps even prevented my daily burnout from spiraling into one big terrible ball of darkness.

If your story causes you to struggle or experience emotional pain, makes you feel "less than," or gets in the way of using your full capacity to work toward your goals and thrive, it is not a helpful story. And you need to tap into your courage to edit it.

As I mentioned, you're going to be practicing many different ways of editing the stories your brain tells you throughout your Awesome Human Project. (You've already begun to do it with your Struggle Awareness practice.) Here's your next practice.

PRACTICE

Edit Your Story

Step 1: Identify a few stories you've always believed about yourself that cause you to struggle.

> What is something you've always believed that makes you feel bad about yourself?

> What assumptions do you make about yourself that cause you to feel stressed, overwhelmed, or anxious?

> What are some things you believe others expect of you that cause you to feel pressured or not good enough?

Jot down your answers to these questions. Read what you wrote, and pick one story to focus on for this practice. I'm sure you have a lot of material to work with—our brains are great creative writers!—but start with just one. You can always come back and do this practice for your other stories.

Step 2: Ask: Is this story true?

Write down facts that support this story, and please remember that what you think or what you think other people think doesn't qualify as a fact. A fact is something you can substantiate with actual evidence of how it's true. Then write down facts that counter the story. This second part will be more challenging, but please spend some time and effort thinking back through your life experience to come up with these.

Look at both sets of facts. Does seeing them side by side introduce some doubt into how much you believe your story?

Step 3: Ask: Is this story helpful?

Does this story energize and motivate you?

Does it make it harder or easier for you to do the hard things you do every day?

Does it help you be a better human being, parent, friend, colleague, leader, or student?

How does believing in this story help or prevent you from achieving goals that are meaningful to you?

Remember that it's taken your whole lifetime until now to create this story, so don't expect to just eliminate it with one practice. The purpose of this practice is to become more aware of the unhelpful stories your brain tells you and get more skilled at editing them rather than just accepting them as fact.

Growing Your Courage

I'm not going to lie to you: facing your stories can be overwhelming and scary. Even as my burnout became all-encompassing and it was clear something needed to change, I was still scared to let go of my story that I was a superwoman and a tough cookie. I didn't have the courage to admit I needed help.

OMG, how could someone like me need help!

Of course, my friends, colleagues, and husband had all tried to suggest that I should get some help. I refused. When one of my investors, also a friend, gave me an ultimatum to go see a certain woman named Janet or he would not talk to me again, I felt so much shame. It felt like confirmation that I'd failed at life and that the story I had believed about myself being a force of nature who could persevere through anything was a lie.

I went to see Janet after kicking and screaming inside for a few months, and she eventually became my spiritual teacher and helped guide me through the worst of my burnout and beyond. (This happened only because she was really smart and never used the word *spiritual* for the first year because I was in no way ready to open up to the idea that there was a spiritual component to me or my life.) I wasn't aware of it at the time, but it took a lot of *courage* to go see her; to open up and share some of my struggles with her; and to face my shame and recognize that it, too, was based on a false story my brain had made up about me being a superhuman who needed to do everything on my own.

Many of us believe the story that asking for help is a sign of weakness when it's actually a sign of our humanity. If you're struggling, and your brain is shaming you into not getting help because it believes this story, tap into your courage to make cracks in it. You don't have to eliminate it right away, but just take a few steps forward and ask for help. Maybe you begin by opening up to a friend or a family member, or maybe you talk to a therapist, a counselor, or someone in your religious community. It will feel scary, but as I learned, your courage will grow bigger than your fear as you recognize that getting help is the only way to honor what's meaningful to you—and as you begin to feel hope.

Courage, like confidence, isn't something you need to have before you do the thing that requires it. You develop it in the process, in the doing of the hard thing.

Here's my absolute favorite definition of courage. It comes from Alfred Adler, a prominent Austrian psychotherapist and founder of the school of individual psychology. I can unequivocally say that my understanding of courage and my emphasis on it as part of embracing your Awesome Human has been directly influenced by Adler, whom I consider my teacher even though we've obviously never met.

Courage is not an ability one either possesses or lacks. Courage is the willingness to engage in a risk-taking behavior regardless of whether the consequences are unknown or possibly adverse. We are capable of courageous behavior provided we are willing to engage in it. Given that life offers few guarantees, all living requires risk-taking.

You develop courage by doing things that require it.

Kerri is a primary care physician at Massachusetts General Hospital, where she also leads the Center for Physician Well-Being. We met and became friends after I reached out to do some sessions on emotional fitness skills for hospital staff (and, in the interest of full disclosure, Kerri also became my doctor).

What I didn't know when we met—and what you wouldn't know from her generously kind smile and calm, warm nature—is that just two years before, Kerri had lost her son, Colin, in a tragic accident. Her nanny was out for a walk with Colin and his sister when two cars crashed in the street and one of them flew onto the sidewalk, severely injuring the little girl and ending Colin's life. He was just shy of turning three years old.

As a mom, I can't imagine what Kerri went through or how she managed to survive.

"My husband and I felt so powerless in the days and weeks after the accident," Kerri said. "We were paralyzed with grief, and I was afraid to even think about feeling less grief because grief was my relationship with Colin.

"But Colin had brought us so much happiness during his short life on earth that I made him a promise that somehow we would find our way there again—to being able to feel joy. I had no idea how we would do it, but I just put one foot in front of the other and tried to make it moment by moment. I would tell myself 'Okay, Kerri, get out of bed. Okay, stir the pasta, and then you can collapse, but stir the pasta for now.'"

It took a long time, but Kerri shared that slowly some color began to return to her life. She and her husband found ways to feel some joy along with their unimaginable sadness and grief. They found ways to honor Colin's memory by creating new memories with their daughter, and they founded Colin's Joy Project, a nonprofit with the mission to bring joy into the lives of families in their local community.

Kerri didn't know how she would make it through what to a parent is the worst and most unimaginable horror. But she took steps—baby steps at first and then bigger steps—and along the way found courage not just to survive but to find meaning in a tragedy and new joy in her life.

You have this courage within you, too. Although I hope you will never, ever have to reach for it to pull you through something as devastating as what Kerri went through, you have the capacity to grow your courage by doing things that require it.

Here's something really important to understand about courage:

Courage doesn't require that you get rid of fear.

In fact, I think one of the worst pieces of advice ever in the history of all advice is "Be fearless!"

Telling people to be fearless is like telling them not to laugh when they hear a really funny joke. Laughter is a natural human response to hearing something funny. Fear is a natural human response to encountering something unfamiliar, challenging, or uncertain.

Making the choice to engage with a challenging, new, or difficult situation doesn't require that you get rid of fear. It's not actually something you *can* do. What it does require is that you tap into your courage and do the thing *while* you feel fear.

As Mark Twain said, *"Courage is . . . mastery of fear—not absence of fear."*

Courage helps you master your fear. The fear doesn't disappear, but your courage grows to be more powerful than your fear.

NOTE TO SELF

Stop trying to be fearless.

Start doing the thing that scares you and your _courage_ will grow to be bigger than your fear.

How to Talk Back to Your Brain When It's Afraid

As you've already learned, when your brain feels fear because it senses possible danger, it can think all kinds of unhelpful thoughts that cause you to struggle, stress out, and feel anxious. So, one of the things you'll be getting really good at during your Awesome Human Project is learning how to talk back to your brain to help it feel less afraid.

Think of your brain as a small child.

When a small child gets scared of the imaginary monsters in her closet, you don't yell at her to stop being scared, tell her to toughen up, or say she is stupid for thinking that monsters exist. You comfort her and tell her you understand that she is scared. You reassure her by turning on the lights and showing her that there are no monsters in the closet (the light of awareness!). You check that the windows are closed so she can feel safer that no monsters can sneak in. You remind her that when she was afraid of monsters a few nights earlier, they weren't in her room, and she went back to sleep.

This is the approach I want you to practice when you talk back to your brain: treat your brain like a small child who is scared, reassure it by pointing out why its fears might not be true, and shift its attention to something more productive and helpful. And please put on your bossy pants and do this with confidence—no waffling about when you're talking back to your brain!

Here's a practice to give it a try.

PRACTICE

Talk Back to Your Brain

Use this practice when your brain offers you a thought that causes you to struggle and feel stressed or overwhelmed.

First, think about what might be causing your brain to be scared:

Is it afraid of how you or someone else will respond to the situation?

Is it focused on the worst-case scenario because of its negativity bias?

Is it afraid because the outcome is uncertain?

Is your brain making assumptions about what others think or feel about you?

This step requires some courage because you have to be vulnerable to be honest with yourself about your fears. But it's really important to become aware of the fear at the root of your brain's stress or worry. So don't slight this part of the practice.

Next, talk back to your brain. (Remember your bossy pants!)

Always acknowledge and calm its fear first, just like you would for a small child, by pointing out how its fear might be unfounded.

Remind it why this thought is not helpful to you.

Redirect its attention to something specific that would be helpful to you in this particular situation.

Here are a few examples of what talking back to your brain might look like:

Fear-Based Thought	Talk Back to Your Brain Script
I feel really guilty that I have to work a lot. My kid got a bruise, and I feel like if I had been there, it wouldn't have happened. FEAR: My kid will think I'm a bad mom because I didn't prevent him from falling and I can't protect him from pain.	Dear Brain, I know you're afraid that my son won't love me as much because I wasn't there to protect him. Maybe you're also afraid that I can't be there to protect him from future bruises—physical or emotional. But kids fall; it's what happens! My son is fine. And get real: it's not realistic to think I can always be there to protect him! So enough with the guilt trip, and let's think about something fun I can do with him this weekend instead.
I'm never going to get all this work done. There's just too much, and I never get stuff done on time anyway. FEAR: Failing to meet expectations and judging yourself harshly when you don't	Dear Brain, My to-do list is long, and you're afraid to disappoint people who depend on me for getting this stuff done. I get it. But please remember that it won't be the end of the world if not every to-do is finished, and stop freaking me out. Let's prioritize my to-do list so I can focus on the most important stuff first. And let's also see if there is anything on there that I can move 'til later or ask someone else to do.

I'm never going to get this job. I'm not qualified enough, and it's way out of my reach. So why bother applying?

FEAR: How badly it will hurt if you're rejected and what others might think

Dear Brain,
You know how much I want this job, and you're afraid of how hurt and disappointed I'll feel if I don't get it. And you're probably afraid of what other people might think if I have to tell them I didn't get it.
  But I've done hard things before, remember? I can handle disappointment, and I will feel good knowing I went for it even when it was challenging.
  So instead of telling me about all the ways I'm not qualified, which makes me feel like crap, let's go over all the awesome strengths I bring as a candidate.

You're going to be talking back to your brain a LOT during your Awesome Human Project. (I do it several times a day still!)

Just because you show your small child there are no monsters in the closet doesn't mean she won't ever get scared again. She will, and she might cry or scream when that happens. Even as you begin to poke holes in your brain's unhelpful stories and talk back to it, it will keep getting scared and reacting in familiar ways—with its negativity bias, worst-case scenarios about the future, and trying to pull you back to the "safety" of the same old story. (Think of these as your brain's version of crying or throwing a tantrum.)

Your job is to keep at it, courageously, firmly, but with compassion and understanding that your brain is scared of new, uncertain, and challenging situations because they might signal danger.

The more you practice, the more instinctual talking to your brain will become. It took tens of thousands of years for the brain to evolve as it has, so you're not going to reverse its tendencies in one lifetime (nor would you want to because, hey, looking out for danger to keep you alive is still really, really useful!). But with consistent practice, you'll help your brain feel less fear and become a much more willing partner in helping you struggle less and grow into a fuller, awesomer version of yourself, a.k.a. your Awesome Human.

Practices In This Chapter

Edit Your Story
Talk Back to Your Brain

Your Note to Self

As you've seen, I'm leaving you some Notes to Self throughout this book to highlight some of the key ideas and concepts I want you to remember. I hope you find them helpful, but what will be *more* helpful is for you to write your own Notes to Self. We remember things better when we summarize and capture them in some way, so at the end of every chapter, I'm going to ask you to write a Note to Self about one thing you want to take away, remember, practice, or reflect on.

You can write your Notes to Self on sticky notes, index cards, in a journal or ninety-nine-cent notebook, or in a Notes app on your computer. You can even email them to yourself if you like, and then put them in a Notes to Self folder you can revisit when you need some Awesome Human reminders. I don't care how you do it but just that you do it.

Keep these short. I say this as someone who is very wordy (I had to cut twenty-five thousand words from my original manuscript of this book because it was too long!), but when you keep them short, you're more likely to remember what you write. And that's really the point: for you to take some time to reflect on everything you're learning as part of your Awesome Human Project, and make it your own.

So, take a moment right now and write your first Note to Self.

What is something you want to remember, practice, or reflect on from this chapter?

AWESOME HUMAN AWARD

After you've done the Edit Your Story practice and practiced talking back to your brain a few times, give yourself the **Not Afraid to Talk Back to My Brain!** award. You so deserve it.

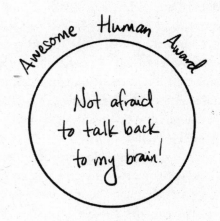

CHAPTER 5

The Surprising Power of Self-Compassion

Awesome Human Quality: Self-Compassion

I'd like you to take a moment and answer this question:

What kind of relationship do you have with yourself?

No, seriously, please stop reading these words and answer the question.

(I'll wait.)

If this question seems odd or makes you uncomfortable, you are not alone.

When I began to ask it during my talks and workshops a few years ago, I had no idea it would stump so many people. The most common response I hear is "I've never thought about this before. . . . I'm not sure."

I also never thought about my relationship with myself until my teacher Janet suggested I try being kinder to myself.

Umm, what?!

My immediate response to her was that I didn't deserve to be kind to myself.

I had obviously failed at life and being an entrepreneur, a leader, and a worthwhile human being because here I was, sitting in a chair across from her, having put my life on hold because I burned out and couldn't function. I had made a bajillion mistakes and hurt some people in the process, including people I loved and teams I cared about.

What I deserved was my own harsh judgment, not kindness. Of this I was certain.

Does this sound familiar?

Perhaps your relationship with yourself is that of a tough critic, always looking for ways you're imperfect, doing something wrong, or not as good as someone else. Or maybe you treat yourself as a tough military sergeant would treat a soldier, giving commands and expecting yourself to execute them perfectly no matter what is going on in your life, how tired you might be, or how unreasonable those commands are.

It's mind-boggling how harsh we can be toward ourselves and how deeply ingrained this harshness is for many of us, isn't it?

We believe that being kind to ourselves is something we need to earn, to deserve, to be "good enough" for, and until we get there, we treat ourselves with so little care and love that if we treated friends that way, well, they wouldn't be our friends for too long.

When, as I was beginning to work my way through my burnout, my teacher suggested that I should be kinder to myself, it seemed almost . . . absurd. I had literally never considered it before, and it felt "correct" that I should withhold kindness and love from myself until I became some version of a perfect human who didn't make mistakes, made every relationship and effort work out in the best possible way, and achieved every big and bold goal I'd set for myself.

Janet didn't seem to care about any of it. So I'd made some mistakes, done things that did not work out, and was completely burned out because I'd pushed myself so hard my whole life. None of this was reason to withhold kindness from myself, according to my teacher. It was evidence of my becoming a human being.

I'll spare you the many arguments I used to try to counter what she said. My brain had me convinced that although others deserved to treat themselves with compassion, I certainly didn't. And I didn't for a moment consider that decades of self-harshness had anything to do with my burnout.

But there was a crack in my stubbornness. And here's the thing I realized, even though I really hated this realization:

My teacher didn't make the crack. I did, and she simply shed some light on it. I already knew, deep down—really deep down!—that I needed to improve my relationship with myself.

You have this wisdom, too.

Even if you've spent most of your life treating every mistake you've made as a mortal sin and punishing yourself for it. Or being the harshest self-critic. Or believing that you don't deserve your own kindness because you've not achieved or done enough or aren't good enough as a person, leader, or parent.

You know. Deep down, you *know* that treating yourself with harshness or endless criticism doesn't actually help you improve, grow, do your work, or live your life in a more meaningful and satisfying way. It steals your joy, adds stress, and drains your energy.

Deep down you know that you need to treat yourself with more kindness and compassion.

What Does Self-Compassion Actually Mean?

It's actually quite simple. And you already know how to do it.

Just think about how you treat your friends and people you care about.

When they make a mistake, my bet is that you don't call them pathetic or stupid or tell them how this mistake makes them a terrible human being. You probably hear them out; acknowledge that maybe that was not the best way to handle the situation; and then encourage them not to beat themselves up, to learn from it, and to move on.

Contrast this with the way you treat yourself when you make a mistake. (This will sting, I know.)

Or, say, a friend tells you she is exhausted from working nonstop. What do you say? *Suck it up; don't be so pathetic; rest is for the weak so just tough it out and keep going!* No, never. I am certain of it. But my bet is that you've said something similar to yourself on more than one occasion.

You treat your friends with care, compassion, and inherent recognition that they are human beings who can't always do everything 1,000 percent super-duper correctly without ever making a mistake—or push themselves to the brink every single day without ever needing a break. In your interactions with them, your goal is to encourage and support them, not make them feel like crap.

This is what it means to treat yourself with compassion: **to recognize that you're a human being who can't always achieve perfection and to approach yourself in a supportive, caring way that aims to reduce struggle and suffering.** In other words, treat yourself as you would a friend.

If this sounds challenging, I get it. Being kind to others seems to come more naturally to most of us than being kind to ourselves.

I've asked hundreds of people about why they withhold compassion from themselves, and here's the most common answer:

"I'm afraid if I treat myself with compassion, I won't ever be motivated to improve. My self-criticism is what helps me get better."

This was absolutely my fear, too, so I am really excited to bust right through it! (Here's a spoiler alert: zero studies show that harsh self-criticism helps you improve. Zero.)

First things first: **Treating yourself with compassion doesn't mean ignoring your flaws, mistakes, or failures!**

Actually, it's the opposite.

Self-compassion asks you to have the *courage* to witness yourself fully and clearly with all the mistakes, flaws, and imperfections, without judging yourself for having them, pretending you don't have them, or thinking you're the only person in the world who has them.

(Gasp! I know, I know. My name is Nataly, and I am a recovering perfectionist. Accepting that I am not and will never be perfect is not an easy feat for me. If it's not for you, either, welcome to the club.)

To witness means to notice, observe, and acknowledge how something is. *This is how this is.*

To judge means to have an opinion or make a decision about how and why something is. *I hate how this is, and because it's like this, here's what it means.*

Witnessing focuses your mind on the facts. But when you judge yourself, your brain makes up a deterministic, negative, and often overblown story about the facts. Remember what you learned about your brain in chapter 3, "Meet Your Brain on Challenge"? All of those tendencies—negativity bias, fear of uncertainty, and defaulting to familiar thinking patterns—come into play when you're judging yourself.

Here are a few examples of the difference between judging and witnessing:

Judging	Witnessing
I messed up this recipe because I'm a terrible cook.	I messed up this recipe.
I'm so fat because I have zero willpower and discipline.	I have fifteen pounds to lose to be at a healthy weight.
I yelled at my child; I'm such an awful mom.	I yelled at my child.

| If my work was any good, I would be further along in my career, so I must be no good. | I've not gone as far in my career as I'd like to. |

Self-compassion asks you to shift from judging yourself to witnessing yourself. This is a perfect opportunity to exercise your thought-editing skills: keep the facts and discard the stories your brain has made up about the facts.

I'll take it further (and this is probably the hardest part): self-compassion involves not just witnessing yourself as you are but accepting yourself as you are.

Okay, Nataly, now that's just crazy talk. How can I accept myself when there are so many things I want to change and improve?!

I hear you. Acceptance is such a tricky concept, and it's the first skill you'll be practicing during your Five-Week Emotional Fitness Challenge. But for now, read this twice:

Accepting yourself as you are right now doesn't mean you don't work to improve!

And once more, with feeling: Accepting yourself as you are right now doesn't mean you don't work to improve!

When you accept yourself as you are, flaws and awesomeness and everything in between, you're not saying, *Okay, great, never change or improve and be a lazy sloth for the rest of your life!* You're simply *witnessing* how you are *right now* with mindfulness instead of *judging* how you are with harshness.

Self-acceptance is not the end. It's the beginning. It's the starting point to improving, growing, and evolving. It allows you to do the work to improve from a place of love versus judgment, harshness, or fear of not being good enough.

And when you begin from a place of love and respect for yourself, you're much more likely to achieve your goals. That's because treating yourself with self-compassion reduces unnecessary struggle, so you have more emotional and mental energy to do the work to improve and grow in meaningful ways.

Your harsh thoughts of self-judgment and self-criticism aren't free! Every thought you think either drains your energy or fuels it, and we can agree that self-criticism isn't energizing. So when you berate yourself, you literally drain the emotional and mental energy you could be using to help you improve or, say, get through your day and tackle that very long to-do list.

How Self-Compassion Helps You Improve

It turns out that self-compassion isn't an impediment to self-improvement—it's a necessary, non-negotiable ingredient of it.

Studies have shown that when people react with self-compassion to making a mistake or failing at something, they are more likely to work harder and do better on the same task next time.

Researchers have even found that self-compassion works better as a source of motivation than boosting your self-esteem (e.g., telling yourself you're completely and utterly awesome). And like I told you before: not a single study has found that endlessly criticizing yourself helps you to improve.

When you courageously witness and accept yourself as you are—including areas you want to improve—rather than judge and criticize yourself, you reduce struggle and have more energy and clarity of mind to identify ways to move forward, grow, and improve. And you actually feel motivated to do it because you haven't painted yourself into an inescapable corner with judgment!

I have fifteen pounds to lose to be at a healthy weight is a starting point from which you can take some actions. For example, you might identify a few ways you can add healthy foods into your diet to substitute for the less healthy ones, or try a new workout.

I'm so fat because I have zero willpower and discipline doesn't leave you anywhere to go. You've determined that you have zero willpower and discipline, so why try anything? Why bother? This is another example of a defeatist and unhelpful story your brain has created that you need to bust through so you can actually take a step forward. (If you find yourself trapped in a similar self-defeating story, go back and do the Edit Your Story practice.)

NOTE TO SELF

Self-compassion helps you improve because instead of wasting energy beating yourself up you can use it to do the improving.

The other reason self-compassion increases your motivation to improve is because it reduces your fear of making mistakes.

If you know you won't beat yourself up if you make a mistake and instead support yourself as you learn from it, you will be less afraid of making it. The more you practice self-compassion when you make a mistake, the safer your brain will feel and the more courage you'll have to risk making mistakes.

You know this instinctively when it comes to people you love: when a friend makes a mistake, you don't go yelling criticisms at her because you know it's only going to make her feel worse. But if you're a good friend, you also don't ignore her mistake or tell her to forget it completely. You acknowledge the mistake, and you offer support and perhaps even a way to move forward. This is how I am asking you to practice reacting to your own mistakes—with compassion.

Shifting from Harsh to Kind Self-Talk

Read these two statements:

I can't believe you screwed that up so badly! You always find a way to screw up; it's like you can't do anything right to save your life! How could you blurt that out in front of the client? You're really, really stupid.

Okay, that was not the best thing to say in the meeting, and you probably could have done it better. But it was a really stressful situation, and it made it hard to think clearly on the spot. Don't beat yourself up about it—you're a human being, not some perfection machine. Now you know for next time that when you're stressed out in a client meeting, count to three in your head before saying anything, just in case.

Which one makes you feel motivated to improve going forward?

It's a silly question because the answer is so obvious—of course, it's the second one. Even writing the first statement made me feel like crap. And feeling like crap is never motivating.

In the second statement, you're doing three things:

1. You're acknowledging the situation and how you did (witnessing instead of judging).

2. You're saying something supportive and reminding yourself that perfection is not possible and mistakes happen.

3. You're identifying one thing you can do better next time in a similar situation.

I call this my little ASM framework: **Acknowledge. Support. Move Forward.** I bet you're already using it when talking to your friends, without even knowing it. Here's how you can put it into practice to shift from harsh to kinder self-talk.

PRACTICE

Three Steps to Talking to Yourself Like a Friend

When you've made a mistake or didn't handle something as well as you would have liked, and you notice that your brain is talking to you in a harsh way, imagine that this happened to a good friend and you're talking to her about it.

Step 1: **Acknowledge.** Acknowledge the situation or the mistake fully but without judgment. (Remember that you're talking to someone you really care about.)

Step 2: **Support.** Say something supportive. It can be a reminder that no one is perfect, you're human, and this wasn't the worst possible thing in the world.

Step 3: **Move forward.** Identify one specific step to move forward (e.g., what lesson can be learned, how can this be avoided in the future, or what can be done to make the situation a little better).

Here are a few examples of reframing harsh self-judgments into talking to yourself as a friend:

Talking to Yourself Like a Harsh Judge	Talking to Yourself Like a Caring Friend
"I'm such an idiot that I forgot to do X!"	"You had a lot going on, so you forgot to do X. It's okay; it happens. Why don't you set a reminder on your phone next time so you don't forget?"
"I'm so lazy! I didn't even get half the stuff done today that I planned!"	"It was unrealistic to think you could get all that done in a day—that list was crazy long. But you got a bunch accomplished, and you have your list ready to tackle for tomorrow."
"I sounded so dumb in that meeting! I can't believe I didn't remember all the stats I should know by heart!"	"That was a really stressful meeting, and you didn't do your best. It happens, and it wasn't the worst thing in the world. Why not follow up with everyone by email to share the stats?"
"Ugh, if (insert name of colleague) was doing this pitch, she would nail it. I suck compared to her."	"If you get stuck in comparison mode, you'll just waste your energy. Remember how many pitches you've nailed before and why you're excited to give this one!"

"I'm a terrible dad—I was so distracted with work during dinner, and now my kids hate me for ignoring them."

"Okay, so maybe you were distracted, and it was less than ideal. But this is just one dinner, and your project is nuts right now. Why don't you make tomorrow's dinner a little special in some way?"

Notice that I'm asking you to use "you" when you practice talking to yourself as a friend. Research shows that when you talk to yourself in the second person, using "you" or your name, your positive self-talk is more impactful than when you use "I" because addressing yourself as another person allows you to be more objective. Research also shows that talking to yourself in a supportive way has the same impact as when a friend is supportive of you.

This is why this three-step practice is so powerful: it puts you in the position of being an objective, supportive friend who helps you move through a tough situation versus getting stuck wasting your energy on self-criticism.

And while we're on the topic of shifting out of harsh self-talk, may I suggest some words to use less often? And by "may I?" I mean that I am strongly encouraging you to swap some words that only increase pressure, stress, and struggle for words that give you some breathing room—less talking to yourself like a machine and more like a human being.

Less	More
Always	Often
I must	I will
Should	Could
Every	Most of the time

The other day, I got a memory from Facebook, a post I made twelve years ago: *"Decided to get up every single day at 6 a.m. and go to the gym. Let's see how this goes!"* I felt so much compassion for the younger me because I could literally feel my own toughness and expectations of perfection in my words. There's nothing wrong with getting up early to work out—it's awesome!—but give yourself some breathing room with your commitments, will you?

How to Stop Buying the Story of "I'm Not Enough"

One of the most common ways our brain's self-criticism causes us to struggle is to replay stories of how we're not good enough:

My work is not good enough, and I won't get promoted.

I'm not technical enough to do great at my project management job.

I'm not a good enough parent.

I'm not fit enough, and I'll never lose the weight I want to lose.

I'm not successful enough professionally.

My writing is not good enough, and I won't ever finish my novel.

I'm not adult enough because I'm thirty years old and still live with my parents.

It's as if the brain thinks that by telling us all the ways we're not good enough, it will motivate us to be better. No way. Just think about how your brain's "not-good-enough" stories make you feel.

One of my brain's favorite "not-good-enough" stories has to do with my work. My brain loves to make me doubt myself and tell me, "My work isn't original enough, and other great minds have already said all there is to say on these topics, and why do I think what I teach is unique in any way?" You know what I feel like when I listen to these stories?

Deflated. Terrible. The opposite of motivated. Small. In no way inspired to write, teach, speak, or learn anything new.

Enough with the not good enough!

It's time to call BS on your brain and the story it keeps telling you about all the ways you're not good enough, not successful enough, not this or that enough.

Seriously.

NOTE TO SELF

Sometimes you just have to call B.S. on your brain's "not good enough" stories. Yes. Really.

Here's a practice to help you do it that's a version of the Edit Your Story practice from chapter 4, on courage.

PRACTICE

Call B.S. on Your "Not Good Enough"

Pick one "not-good-enough" story your brain is telling you. Maybe it's the one you hear most frequently or the one that's loudest.

Next, take out a piece of paper and write this story at the top. Then create two columns: *Facts That Support/Facts That Counter.*

In the first column, write down facts that support your not-good-enough story. Please remember that what you think or what you assume someone else thinks is not a fact. A fact has to be something you *know* to be true; no cheating (e.g., "I think my boss thinks I'm not good at my job" is not a fact, but "I got negative feedback on x, y, z" is).

In the second column, write down facts that counter your story. For example, if your story is that you're not good enough at your job, facts that counter it are positive comments from your boss, coworkers, or clients; good reviews or promotions; challenges you've worked through successfully; or ways you've helped colleagues that were meaningful or contributed to your team/organization. (Warning: your brain is going to try to stop you from coming up with these. Keep at it.)

After you've written out both sets of facts, take a step back and look at your columns: *Which one has more facts in it? Which side is more convincing? What parts of the story can you discard, and what are some things you might learn to help you move forward with less struggle?*

I've done this practice with many Awesome Humans, and it's really powerful to witness them find cracks in their "not-good-enough" stories. I'm not going to promise you that doing this once will free you from the hold of your "not-good-enough" story, especially if it's one you've believed for some time. But a crack is an opening that creates an opportunity for you to tell a better, more helpful story, one that allows you to embrace and share your Awesome Human with the world.

In fact, as you get more honest about your story through this practice, you might discover that some aspects of it *are* true. Not the "you're not good enough so feel crappy about yourself" parts—never!—but parts you can learn from. For example, "I'm not technical enough to succeed in my job" might evolve into a much more helpful version of "I want to get more confidence around my technical skills so I need to take some extra courses." Think about how much more possibility, motivation, and fuel there is in the new version of this story!

AWESOME HUMAN AWARD

Learning to avoid going along with your brain's "not-good-enough" stories is one of the toughest skills to master, so after you do this practice a few times and begin to feel like you're getting the hang of it, give yourself the **Calling BS on My Brain's "Not-Good-Enough" Stories** award!

We can't talk about feeling not good enough without talking about imposter syndrome for a moment. Imposter syndrome is that nagging feeling that you're not as good as other people think you are and that sooner or later, they will come to their senses and realize this. Maybe you feel that you don't deserve to be where you are and that you got there by mistake.

This recently came up in my conversation with Jodi, one of the leaders I work with. She has reached a senior level at her company but told me that she couldn't shake the feeling that she wasn't good enough to be there. I asked her if she has gotten any feedback to indicate that her superiors weren't happy with her performance, and she told me that no, it's actually been the opposite—she's gotten some great feedback.

"So you think they are all stupid, then—is that right?" I asked her.

"No, I respect them; they are smart people. I like working with them," she answered.

"Well, if they have hired you, promoted you, and given you positive feedback when you actually suck at your job, that means they are stupid!"

Jodi laughed. This was a ridiculous statement, but it was a helpful one. It highlighted a flaw in her imposter syndrome: if people whose judgment she trusted made the decisions to hire her, promote her, and give her positive feedback, then how could it be true that she wasn't good enough for her job? She either had to believe they were stupid and had no idea what they were doing or her brain's "not-good-enough" story was BS.

Until my conversation with Jodi, I hadn't fully recognized this aspect of imposter syndrome: it's arrogant in its assumption that other people are wrong about us. I've dealt with my share of imposter syndrome throughout my career, and this insight was a big one for me. So the next time your brain is trying to convince you that you're not as good as others think you are, ask yourself: *Are they stupid?* This is a humbling but incredibly helpful question. Truly, give it a shot.

Learning to Forgive Yourself

I saved what might be the toughest part of practicing self-compassion for last. But it's also often the most powerful: learning to forgive yourself.

For most of my life, I believed that you pay for mistakes with guilt. I would relive moments when I felt I had done something wrong over and over in my mind, feeling guilty and blaming myself for not having handled things better.

Like the time I dropped off my daughter at preschool and forgot to wave good-bye to her at our usual good-bye window. She got so upset that her teachers had to call me to come back, and it broke my heart to see her sobbing. I could hardly function for the rest of the day, although when

I picked her up later, she didn't even remember that it had happened. She is seventeen years old now, and I still sometimes feel guilty about that day!

Or the times I didn't acknowledge the challenges we were having as a team at work or open up about my own struggles, trying to pretend everything was great and cheerlead the team through what obviously was a difficult time everyone needed to address.

Or the times my husband tried to help me out of the Valley of Struggle, and I yelled at him for being shallow and not feeling my pain enough.

I've relived these and many other moments and mistakes so often, beating myself up, wishing I had done better. My guilt would often overwhelm me and make me feel trapped: I couldn't go back and fix things and yet I couldn't shake the heavy feeling of guilt.

The idea to forgive myself never crossed my mind.

But guilt doesn't reach into the past and change it or help you avoid making mistakes in the future. It traps you, and it drains your emotional and mental energy. The same energy you could be using to do something kind, supportive, or meaningful for other people. The same energy you could use to learn something about your guilt that would actually help you avoid making the same mistakes.

Susan David, author of *Emotional Agility*, talks about our feelings being signposts. This is such a useful perspective. When you have a feeling like guilt, approach it with curiosity to see what you can learn from it, and then use that learning to move forward and do better.

What can I learn from feeling guilty about not waving to Mia at the good-bye window? I love her so much . . . and it's important to me to be present when we're together. Focusing on this versus my guilt helps me think of ways I can be more present, like putting away my phone when we're hanging out (unless we're taking silly selfies, obviously).

Here are two questions I find helpful to ask when I get stuck in guilt and have a hard time forgiving myself:

- How is staying trapped in guilt helpful (to me, the person I feel I wronged, or other people in my life)?

- What can I learn from feeling guilty about this (and how can I use it to do better going forward)?

I encourage you to practice asking these questions when you get stuck in guilt and have a difficult time forgiving yourself. If you can be honest about your answers, they will guide you through.

Sometimes it's not the guilt over something you've done to others but not being able to forgive yourself for choices or decisions you made in the past that keeps you stuck in struggle. The negativity bias in your brain is strong, and your brain is so good at remembering and reminding you of all the things you've done wrong—or it's decided that you've done wrong. And if you've been playing these self-critical stories on repeat for decades, it's going to take a lot of practice to interrupt the cycle.

But you can do it. And the way to do it is to practice seeing yourself through the eyes of someone who loves you.

Before I share a practice to help you do this, I want to tell you about the woman who inspired it. One time, I was teaching a virtual workshop on creativity to a group of employees at Google. As part of it, I led everyone in a little watercolor-painting session. Most participants had never tried watercolor before, and one of my goals for asking them to do this was to practice quieting their inner critic.

At the end of the workshop, I asked if people wanted to share their artwork and what went through their minds as they painted. One woman raised her hand and showed everyone her painting of a turtle—it looked so fun and friendly! She said that as she was painting her turtle, her self-critic was in overdrive, telling her how terrible her painting was coming out and how she wasn't creative. Then suddenly, her five-year-old daughter ran up to her, looked at the painting, and told her how much she loved it! The woman, with a tear in her eye, said that in that moment she decided to try looking at herself through the eyes of her daughter every day, especially when her inner critic got loud!

I loved this so much, and I told her that she inspired me to do this more for myself—and to share this idea with as many people as I can.

So here's your final practice for this chapter, and if I could give you a huge hug as you dive into it, I would. Imagine a really warm, virtual hug flying your way instead!

PRACTICE

See Your Past Through the Eyes of Someone Who Loves You

Grab a journal or a piece of paper to do this practice.

Step 1. Think back to your past and zoom in on those times when you feel you made a mistake, failed, or made the wrong choice. Pick one or two to start with.

Write a few sentences about what happened, not editing your thoughts in any way. You've probably thought about this a lot, so write down exactly what you've been thinking.

Step 2. Imagine that a friend, someone who has full knowledge of what happened, is talking about this same situation. Perhaps this friend was there with you during that time. Write down what they would say about it if they were asked to describe it.

Step 3. Compare the two stories: What differences do you notice?

When I've practiced this, my version is full of judgment and harshness, and my friend's is more compassionate, understanding, and focused on what I might have learned versus how badly I should feel about it.

As you read through the two stories, think about which version fuels you with motivation to move forward, learn, and do better and which version drains your energy and deflates you. Just as you get to choose the thoughts you accept from your brain and the thoughts you edit or release, you get to choose the story about your past choices.

I encourage you to choose the one that causes less struggle so you can use that energy to learn, improve, and flourish.

Replace "OR" with "AND"

One of the most powerful lessons I've learned since I began to practice self-compassion is about replacing "or" with "and." (I promise you this is not a grammar lesson.)

I used to think:

I can either treat myself nicely OR work hard.

I can either accept how I am OR improve.

I can either forgive myself OR learn from my mistakes (by constantly replaying them in my mind).

But I was wrong.

When you treat yourself with compassion and care, like you would a friend, you can actually work hard for a sustainable period of time without burning out because you will be supporting yourself rather than being your own drill sergeant.

When you accept yourself as you are, courageously witnessing your awesomeness and ways you want to improve, you're more likely to do what you need to do to get better because you are doing it from a place of love instead of fear of not being good enough.

When you forgive yourself for having made mistakes and learn from them rather than trap yourself in guilt, you're actually more likely not to make the same mistakes in the future.

It turns out that what we think of as trade-offs are actually complementary:

You can treat yourself nicely AND work hard.

You can accept how you are AND improve.

You can forgive yourself AND learn from your mistakes.

Replacing "OR" with "AND" has been a huge, life-changing mindset shift that I encourage—implore? strongly advise while wearing my bossy pants?—you to make.

Practices in This Chapter

Three Steps to Talking to Yourself Like a Friend
Call BS on Your "Not Good Enough"
See Your Past Through the Eyes of Someone Who Loves You

Your Note to Self

What is something you want to remember, practice, or reflect on from this chapter?

AWESOME HUMAN AWARD

Oof, this is a big one: after you've done the practices in this chapter and begun to create a more compassionate relationship with yourself, you wholeheartedly deserve the **In a Committed, Supportive Relationship with My Awesome Self** award!

CHAPTER 6

Your Emotional Whiteboard

Awesome Human Quality:
Emotional Awareness and Openness

What if I told you there's a whiteboard hanging in front of your chest right now?

You'd look down, see no whiteboard, and tell me that I'm making it up.

But let me assure you that it's there. It's your Emotional Whiteboard.

How you feel in this moment, what your energy is like—it's all written on your Emotional Whiteboard. And everyone you interact with throughout your day, from your family members to your colleagues, sees your Emotional Whiteboard, whether you acknowledge it or not.

Remember our Tense Boss meeting scenario? You sensed your boss was stressed without her telling you she was tense. You read these emotions on her Emotional Whiteboard.

As humans, we're really great at communicating our emotions through facial expressions and body language and sensing the emotions of others. This helps us to exchange information really quickly. Say I see you eat something and feel disgusted by it. Your facial expression of disgust can help me avoid eating that horrible thing. But if you eat it and look satisfied, I quickly learn that it's tasty (and safe to eat)!

What's fascinating is that when I observe your reaction of being disgusted—or stressed or joyful—I begin to actually experience that same emotion! This happens because mirror neurons in my brain literally reflect your feelings. My brain doesn't want me to eat that disgusting and potentially dangerous food, so it actually begins to *feel* disgust. On the flip side, if I see you smile after you eat it, my brain makes me smile so that I can be enticed by that positive reaction to partake in whatever yummy thing you discovered.

(Of course, sometimes this leads to unpleasant surprises. I love olives, and I definitely have a look of satisfaction on my face whenever I eat them. When my daughter was younger, she grabbed one after noticing how much I enjoyed them and, oh boy, the look on her face communicated only one thing: *WHAT IS THIS HORRIBLE THING, AND WHY DID YOU LET ME HAVE IT?* She is seventeen now. We are still working on her love of olives. Not much progress, but I'm not giving up.)

Human emotions are literally contagious, which means that people can not only sense what's written on your Emotional Whiteboard but also they can "catch" your feelings.

If you're burning out daily and feeling stressed out, low, or overwhelmed, these are the feelings you're passing on to others. I recognize that this might be painful to hear. But I need you to hear it because it might be the nudge—okay, strong push—you need to make your own well-being and emotional fitness your priority.

You don't just impact others with your words and actions. You impact them with your emotions and your emotional and mental energy, even if you think you're really awesome at hiding how you feel. As hard as you might try, you can't avoid sharing your true feelings with others.

I learned this the hard way.

For most of my career, I prided myself on being amazing at putting on a "confident, positive" mask. I was so sure that even when I was overwhelmed, exhausted, or deep in self-doubt, I could hide it all and show up as the confident and positive leader my team was expecting. (Or rather, that's what I thought they were expecting.)

There's actually a name for pretending to feel good when you don't—it's called surface acting. It's a form of emotional labor that drains a ton of energy, and research suggests it's one of the causes of burnout. I have no doubt that this was true in my case.

But my pretending didn't just hurt me—it also hurt my team. For months before I hit bottom, many of my team members were asking me with increasing frequency if everything was okay or if they could help. They saw the overwhelm, stress, and anxiety all over my Emotional Whiteboard, even though I kept pretending to be okay and telling them everything was fine, which it wasn't, of course.

This disconnect, created by my futile attempts to pretend to be the all-is-great-don't-worry-about-me leader, caused tons of confusion for my team and eroded their trust. My Emotional Whiteboard was filled with so many difficult feelings of doubt, anxiety, dread, and overwhelm, but I never *acknowledged* them. So although my team members sensed I was in bad shape, they didn't know exactly what I was feeling or why.

This is why emotional awareness and openness is an essential Awesome Human Quality. You're always sharing your emotions with others, and you need to become intentional about being aware of what they are and how they impact people around you.

Becoming Aware of How You Feel

You'd think we wouldn't need to practice becoming aware of our own feelings, right?

Wrong. Just as it takes practice to become aware of your thoughts, it takes practice to become aware of your feelings. Feeling something is not the same as knowing what you feel.

Thich Nhat Hanh, one of the most venerable Buddhist teachers, has a very simple breathing meditation I love to practice. As you breathe in, you say to yourself, "I am breathing in," and as you breath out, you say, "I am breathing out." Of course, we breathe all the time but often without awareness. And when we pause to become aware of our breath, our brain catches up to our body and we feel more whole and connected. In the same way, when we become aware of our emotions, we have an opportunity to connect to ourselves.

Before I burned out, I don't remember ever pausing to acknowledge my feelings. Of course, I had many different feelings, but it was almost like *I didn't actually experience* them. My emotional awareness was reserved for peak feelings only, when I was completely overwhelmed with stress or feeling intense joy. The peak feelings were so strong that I didn't have a choice but to be aware of them. But most of the time, I was disconnected from my own emotional experience.

I've often said that I lived most of my life from the neck up.

I grew up in a very loving family, and believe me, we all had big and bold emotions, but we rarely talked about them. We did talk a lot about ideas and knowledge, and I guess I just carried that with me. No one ever told me emotions weren't important, but no one ever taught me they were, either, or how they affected everything and everyone in my life. And I never once worked for or with someone who mentioned feelings in the context of work, so I was convinced they definitely didn't belong there, either.

The concept of becoming aware of what I felt, of acknowledging my feelings and embracing them rather than ignoring them, was completely new to me. And wow, it was hard to practice!

At one point, I attended a meditation workshop, and the Buddhist monk teaching it said, "Meditation is not about getting rid of your thoughts and feelings but about becoming aware of them." I'd never meditated before, and I had this whole story of how I was way too type A for it to work, blah blah blah. But when you get to a really dark place, you become willing to try new things, so I decided to try it.

I remember sitting on a cushion in our little basement room and trying to practice becoming aware of my feelings. After two minutes, all I wanted to do was quit!! I didn't feel calm like all the people in meditation stock photos. I hated ALL the feelings I experienced, and I didn't want to feel them. I just wanted to go back to my emotional oblivion, which I did for a while, until I burned out and had no choice but to feel: all my emotions just poured out, and I couldn't just shove them back down.

My goal isn't to freak you out by sharing this but to acknowledge that emotional awareness can be difficult to practice, and if you stumble or find it challenging, there is nothing wrong with you. You're just a human being trying to do something you haven't done before!

And like anything else, the more you practice, the easier it becomes.

So, how do you go about practicing emotional awareness?

The most helpful thing I did to begin was to make time to be alone and quiet and reflect on how I was feeling.

This sounds simple, but it wasn't. When we pause the hectic pace with which most of us run through our days and turn our attention inward, it can be overwhelming, especially if difficult feelings come up. Do you know that researchers have found that most people would rather experience physical pain than be left alone with their thoughts and emotions?

The hardest emotions to feel and acknowledge are the difficult ones, like sadness, fear, regret, or doubt. Notice how I'm not calling these negative emotions. There are no negative or positive emotions, no wrong or right ones. Some feelings are more difficult, and some are more pleasant, but every single feeling you have is real and valid and deserves your attention and awareness.

This is really important. Given our culture's endless messages to "Be positive! Turn your frown upside down! Find the silver lining!" it's easy to fall into the trap of positivity and believe that you're not supposed to feel "negative" emotions.

But this isn't true: **You are not meant to feel good all the time.**

You're a human being with complex and different emotions, and every single one is right simply because you feel it. Being emotionally fit and healthy doesn't mean you feel positive all the time. It means you learn how to acknowledge and embrace all of your feelings and get through the difficult ones with less struggle.

Don't Run Away from Difficult Feelings

No doubt, difficult feelings aren't pleasant to feel. They often bring discomfort and pain and can be overwhelming. But here's the thing: trying not to feel them doesn't make them go away.

As psychologist Carl Jung once said, *"That which you resist, persists."*

When you try to avoid feeling a difficult emotion or distract yourself with Netflix or numb it with some red wine, your feeling doesn't go anywhere. You might temporarily hide from it, but it will still be there when your attempts to pretend that it's not run out.

By the way, Netflix and too much red wine used to be two of my favorite feeling-numbing mechanisms. We all have them, and I would love for you to get honest with yourself about your knee-jerk reactions when you experience an emotion you don't want to feel. Do you try to distract yourself? Do you try to drown it out? Becoming aware of how you try to avoid challenging feelings is part of your emotional awareness practice.

Just for the record, I think Netflix and red wine are absolutely fabulous, as are dark chocolate, cherries, and a crusty baguette with a thick layer of butter on it. (This is a good time to tell you that I love food, and especially good food, and also especially the food I just listed.) But the question you want to ask yourself is: *Am I doing this because it's fun and relaxing, or am I using this to not feel what I feel?*

Before you get annoyed at me about questioning your Netflix habit, I want to give you some good news. Research shows that when you acknowledge your difficult feelings, you experience them for a shorter time and with less intensity.

A quick neuroscience lesson: when you acknowledge a difficult feeling, you activate your prefrontal cortex, which helps to calm your amygdala and temper the intensity of your emotion. You've already met your amygdala in chapter 3, "Meet Your Brain on Challenge," and know that it's responsible for managing your emotional response. When you acknowledge your difficult feelings by naming them, your prefrontal cortex becomes like a patient kindergarten teacher who helps your overactive amygdala slow down and reduce the intensity of its emotional response.

> ## NOTE TO SELF
>
> One of the most amazing things you can do for your mental health is stop pressuring yourself to feel good all the time.

You'll be practicing different ways to accept and experience your difficult feelings as part of your Five-Week Emotional Fitness Challenge, and I promise you I have a lot more tangible tips and suggestions for you than "just sit with your feelings," which never worked for me.

But right now, I want you to kickstart your emotional awareness practice.

PRACTICE

Emotional Awareness Check-In
(a.k.a. What's on My Emotional Whiteboard?)

To begin, do this once a day, first thing in the morning or toward the end of the day. As you get the hang of this practice, I would love for you to do it a few times a day. But start with once a day and go from there. How about right now? Check in with yourself to see how you're feeling:

It helps to take a few deep breaths so you can arrive where you are (yes, we humans need help to catch up with ourselves).

Ask yourself: *How do I feel right now? What is written on my Emotional Whiteboard?*

Be as specific as possible, and name whatever feelings you notice—remember that you can experience several different emotions at the same time.

Don't try to fix or change anything; just become aware of how you feel.

Focus on your feelings versus the story your brain might be creating around your feelings ("I feel this" versus "I feel this, so it means that").

Practice self-compassion during your check-in, and imagine you're checking in with a friend.

The goal of your check-in is to become aware of how you feel, but you might find that it guides you to do something to support yourself to feel better. That's awesome, but don't pressure yourself into finding a "solution." Your goal is awareness.

Becoming aware of how you feel, even if your feelings are difficult to experience, is one of the most meaningful gifts you can give to yourself. We all check in on our friends, loved ones, and colleagues, and yet we so rarely check in on ourselves. Practicing your check-in is like saying to yourself, "I care about you, and I want to know how you are doing. Your feelings matter."

After you become more aware of how you feel, you can find ways to support yourself, your energy, your emotional fitness, and your well-being. Research shows that people who are emotionally aware experience greater well-being throughout the day. When you know your energy is running low, you can make a choice to do something to fuel yourself—take a break, get a snack, and so forth. But you need to become aware of how you're feeling first, and this is what emotional awareness helps you do.

When I talk about my burnout, people often ask me if I had noticed warning signs. I can easily name them in retrospect: I began to dread my days and resent my work; I withdrew from as many social interactions as possible, struggled to get the simplest things done, zoned out during meetings and times with my daughter, felt exhausted and had low energy all the time, drank too much wine, and slept at most four to five hours a night. But I wasn't aware of these signs at the time because I was disconnected from my feelings and my daily reality. I ran on fumes and had no tools or practices that would nudge me to pause and actually become aware.

Without practicing emotional awareness, you don't give yourself a chance to make changes and support yourself before you burn out. To be clear, burnout is not just an individual problem—how your workplace is structured, how your boss treats you, and the culture within your team can all contribute to burnout. Lack of control over your work or schedule, insufficient rewards, absence of fairness, lack of sense of community, and an unreasonable workload are some of the common causes of burnout, according to Christina Maslach, a professor of psychology at the University of California–Berkeley who has studied burnout extensively. But there are many factors you *can* control—like making sure you do something outside of work to rest and refuel—and practicing emotional awareness will help you get better at knowing how you can support yourself. (Many of the emotional fitness skills you'll be learning in the next part of your Awesome Human Project will help you do it!)

Clarifying Your Emotional Whiteboard (a.k.a. Emotional Openness)

Now that you're on your way to becoming more aware of your emotions, it's time to talk about being more open about them.

You already know that whether you intend to or not, you're always sharing your emotions with others. We can all read each other's Emotional Whiteboards. But emotional openness is about sharing your feelings *intentionally* and putting them in context so other people don't have to waste their energy guessing or making up stories that might not be true.

Other people see your Emotional Whiteboard through foggy glasses—they can kind of make out what it says but not exactly. They *sense* what you feel rather than know it, and *they don't know why you feel the way you do*. If you don't acknowledge your feelings and clear up the fog, you leave them wondering and creating their own scenarios. Remember that their brains have a negativity bias and fear of uncertainty, just like yours, so their scenarios will likely be negative and dramatic.

In the Tense Boss scenario, as soon as you sensed that something was off in your boss's facial expression, your brain went into overdrive with negative stories. Because it sensed something was wrong—danger!—but didn't know exactly what—uncertainty!—your brain made up dramatic stories of how your boss hated your work and you were about to get fired. Your boss's failure to acknowledge what was on her Emotional Whiteboard made your stress skyrocket.

When you don't clarify your Emotional Whiteboard, you're literally making other people struggle.

Not only do you cause other people unnecessary stress but also you might encourage them to react in ways you never intended and wouldn't want.

When I was burning out, I was constantly on edge, and my team members stopped disagreeing with my decisions because they didn't want to add more stress. I can honestly tell you that we wasted hundreds of thousands of dollars going in wrong directions because our communication and collaboration suffered. Some people on my team began to look for other jobs without coming to me to resolve a problem we might have worked out together. My unwillingness to be open about our challenges caused them to make decisions I wished they hadn't—and that caused me more stress and overwhelm.

This is very painful to admit, but in my efforts to pretend to be okay when I wasn't, I created a culture of mistrust and lack of transparency within my team. It hurt our performance, our ability to be at our best, and our joy of working together.

Several years ago, Google conducted a study to understand why some of its teams were more effective than others. The number one factor that made more successful teams awesome? They all had a culture of psychological safety.

Psychological safety means being able to trust that you can take interpersonal risks at work and not be judged by your team members. When you share a new idea with your

NOTE TO SELF

Being more open about your emotions is an act of kindness toward the people you care about.

team members, tell them you're not sure the project you're all working on is heading in the right direction, or open up about a personal challenge, you're taking interpersonal risks. Research has shown that psychological safety increases productivity and collaboration, improves employee well-being, and increases retention and job satisfaction, among many other benefits.

When you work in an environment of psychological safety, you enjoy your work instead of dreading it, and you have closer, more trusting relationships with your coworkers.

We are all parts of teams in our lives.

A family is a team.

A group of friends is a team.

Your colleagues at work are a team.

When you acknowledge what's written on your Emotional Whiteboard, especially if you're dealing with something difficult or know that you're acting "off," not in the way you usually do, you help create trust and openness. You reduce struggle for everyone, including yourself, and you let other people know that they don't need to go through challenges alone.

That is a huge gift.

It Doesn't Take a Lot, But It Means a Lot

I got such a great reminder from my family recently about how much stress we can reduce for others when we clarify what's on our Emotional Whiteboards.

I told my husband and daughter that I was grateful for their patience and flexibility living with me as a creative who has some serious highs and lows. When I'm stuck while working on a new talk or a book, I can be an absolute emotional roller coaster. (I want to tell you that I was originally going to write "emotional nightmare," but I stopped myself. That wasn't a kind thing to say, and I wouldn't say it about a friend. So I went with "emotional roller coaster" instead. Learning to talk to yourself like a friend is all about taking little steps like this.)

"It's actually not such a big deal anymore," my husband said, smiling.

"It used to be really tough because we wouldn't know *why* you would suddenly act like you were angry or be totally silent and sullen. But now you say stuff like 'Guys, I'm losing my mind with this book chapter!' So we know why you might be acting a certain way, and we can stay out of your way or, you know, make you tea and *then* stay out of your way."

I teach this stuff for a living and still I was stunned by how a little effort on my part to be more open about how I was feeling could help people I loved so much struggle a lot less.

In our Tense Boss scenario, imagine how much less stress and anxiety you would have experienced if your boss told you why she was acting tense. Even if what she shared had something to do with you or your work, you would *know* what it was and could save so much energy by not having to guess.

So why didn't she do it? Why don't most of us practice acknowledging what's on our Emotional Whiteboards?

Because it can be really hard to do! When you acknowledge your emotions, you don't know how people will react, and this can feel vulnerable and scary—especially at work and even more if you work in an environment where sharing feelings is as common as seeing pink unicorns. (Qualifier: If you work in a pink unicorn factory, this is an unfair example. Substitute purple elephants.)

How to Practice Sharing Your Emotional Whiteboard at Work (Even When It's Hard)

When I ask people to practice sharing what's on their Emotional Whiteboard with their colleagues, I get a lot of resistance.

"No way can I share how I feel at work—it's just not something that's done where I work, and my colleagues would think I am weird/weak/touchy-feely if I did it."

I get it. But I need to be annoying and remind you that *you are already sharing your feelings with your colleagues!* They sense what you feel, whether you want them to or not. You've already made that choice by being human. Now I'm asking you to practice giving context to your emotions so your colleagues don't have to waste energy trying to figure them out on their own.

Here's a practice I want you to try.

PRACTICE

Share One Sentence from Your Emotional Whiteboard

When your feelings, energy, or stress level are out of the norm or you believe it would be helpful for your colleagues to know how you feel, share one sentence from your Emotional Whiteboard.

One sentence is a frame that helps you to be succinct and not go into an overload of sharing (if you must make it two sentences, go for it; I will hold off the sentence police!).

Share how you're feeling, but don't feel compelled to tell the whole long story about it. You're offering context, not delivering a TED Talk about your feelings.

It might be helpful to say what you'd like the other person to do—just listen, give advice, something else— and it helps to take the burden off them to figure it out.

You don't have to share your Emotional Whiteboard in every single interaction. A good question to ask yourself is this: *If I were in the other person's shoes, would it be helpful to know something about how I'm feeling right now?*

Please remember that you can't control how people will react when you share. They might need time to process, not be comfortable talking about emotions, or simply not know what to say.

Here are a few examples of how you might share one sentence from your Emotional Whiteboard. You can use them like Mad Libs and substitute your own feelings to get started with this practice.

"Just wanted to give you a heads-up that I've had a few tough days personally, and if you're sensing that something is off, that's it. Nothing to worry about, and I don't need to talk about it but just wanted to let you know."

"I didn't get great sleep last night, so I'm really drained. Definitely quieter than usual today, in case I seem off."

"I just want you to know that I had a really stressful meeting earlier, so if you're feeling tension from me, that's why. It would really help me if we could talk through what you want me to focus on today so I can concentrate in the right area."

Kerri, whom you met in chapter 4, told me recently how sharing her Emotional Whiteboard made a stressful morning less overwhelming for her and her colleagues. Her nanny was late, and her husband had left for work, so she rushed to bring her daughter to school. This made her late, and by the time she ran in to meet the residents who would be going on morning rounds with her, she was tense and stressed out to the max.

"So I decided to share my whiteboard so they knew that my acting all out of sorts had nothing to do with them. It felt like a collective exhale! Everyone relaxed immediately. I said that it would help me a ton if we could just have great rounds, and we did!"

By sharing her Emotional Whiteboard, Kerri helped the residents avoid getting stuck in struggle and instead use their energy to do great work. How awesome is that?

I recognize that practicing emotional openness might be new and scary for you. It was for me when I started! But please use your courage and try it. Start by sharing small things with colleagues with whom you feel comfortable, and remember *why* you're doing this: you're not just sharing your feelings but helping them to waste less energy trying to figure out what you feel. It's an act of service and kindness!

Practices in This Chapter
Emotional Awareness Check-In
Share One Sentence from Your Emotional Whiteboard

Your Note to Self
What is something you want to remember, practice, or reflect on from this chapter?

AWESOME HUMAN AWARD

After you've done the practices in this chapter a few times, give yourself the **Courageously Embracing My Feelings** award. You have earned it!

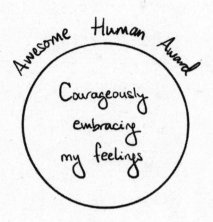

CHAPTER 7

Awesome Humans Are Leaders

Awesome Human Quality: Leadership

Awesome Humans are leaders, not because they manage people or teams or have fancy titles. None of that has anything to do with being a leader, although it's probably how many of us think about it.

I got really curious about the origins of the word *leader*, which sent me down a fascinating rabbit hole of etymology on the internet. I love what I found out.

The word *leader* comes from an Old English word *lædan*, which means "to travel or go somewhere." But *lædan* is what's called a causative form of the verb, which means "cause to do something." So to be a leader is *to cause someone to travel somewhere.*

Although there can be many interpretations, the one most meaningful to me is leadership as causing others to travel within themselves and do the inner work so they can successfully travel outside to the many destinations on their life journey.

So here's my definition of a leader:

To be a leader means to positively impact other people's capacity to thrive.

As a leader, helping people develop their capacity to thrive is your number one intention and your guiding principle for how you interact with others.

A teacher can be a leader.

A coach can be a leader.

A parent can be a leader.

A coworker can be a leader.

You don't need a fancy title, big office, or any direct reports to positively impact others so they can struggle less and thrive more. But you *do* have to be intentional about doing this.

As an Awesome Human, you're a leader because you care about positively impacting other people's capacity to thrive.

To do this, you need to start with yourself. You can't positively impact other people's well-being or their ability to flourish if you don't first improve your own. To be a force of good in the lives of people you care about, you need to practice your emotional fitness skills and develop a supportive, caring relationship with yourself first. And no, there aren't any ways around this.

The Case Against Martyr Leadership

Let me put this more bluntly and directly, just so there's no confusion: I'm asking you to put yourself first by making your well-being and emotional fitness your number one priority.

Did I just trip your "this-is-selfish" alarm?

I realize that the mere suggestion that you should be at the top of your list might run counter to the way you think about being a leader and caring about others.

I, too, always assumed that as a servant leader, my job was to put my needs last and my team's first. I took the old military tradition of "leaders eat last" literally, although in my case it was more like "leaders sleep, rest, and take care of their emotional and mental needs last—or not at all."

I had taken the idea of servant leadership to mean completely the opposite of what it was meant to embody.

Robert K. Greenleaf coined the term *servant leader* in 1970. He described servant leaders as those whose number one priority is to serve others by helping them improve so they can reach their full potential—and so they can eventually become servant leaders themselves. He wrote, "The best test, and difficult to administer, is: Do those served grow as persons? Do they, while being served, become healthier, wiser, freer, more autonomous, more likely themselves to become servants?"

Nowhere in his definition did he talk about servant leaders as those who sacrifice themselves or their emotional health for others.

NOTE TO SELF

To be a leader means to positively impact other people's capacity to thrive.

In fact, it is not possible to practice true servant leadership if you don't invest in your emotional fitness first. **Your emotional fitness as a leader isn't a luxury; it's your responsibility.**

You can't help people improve or be healthier, freer, or wiser if you're constantly stressed out or on the edge of burnout and cause them to struggle because of the emotional confusion and low energy you bring to them (75 percent of US employees say the biggest stress in their lives is their interactions with their boss. Ouch!).

The same is true outside of work: you can't improve the well-being of the people you care about or help them embrace their Awesome Human if you don't embrace your Awesome Human first. It's really tempting to think that you can fake it, but you can't.

You already know that your emotions and energy are contagious. But there's another reason it's absolutely nonnegotiable to do your inner work first:

The way you treat others is rooted in how you treat yourself.

If you're always criticizing yourself, you're likely skilled at criticizing others.

If you don't practice emotional awareness, you're probably not so great at recognizing how others are feeling.

If you expect perfection from yourself, you probably have low tolerance for anything less than perfection in others.

Boy, does this ring true for me. It hurts to write this, but the whole time I thought I was putting my family and my teams first and being a great servant leader, I wasn't. I was impatient, expected perfection, and got stupidly frustrated if it wasn't forthcoming. I wasn't a great listener when someone I cared about shared their struggles because I was so uncomfortable with difficult emotions.

I cared for others deeply and had the most genuine intentions of being a force of good in their lives. But it didn't matter how much I wanted to do this—I couldn't until I began to embrace my Awesome Human and do the inner work myself.

Darin is a friend I met when he reached out to share how my work helped him go from crying daily and feeling no meaning or joy in his life to being fueled with hope and embracing his Awesome Human. I asked him recently if he noticed a change in how he impacts others close to him now, compared with before.

"Oh my goodness," he wrote, "I'm a completely different person. I used to be an uncompromising idealist. If something wasn't a ten out of ten, I'd throw a fit. Everyone else was wrong."

Darin's wife, whom he met as he made progress on his Awesome Human journey, was nearby while we were chatting (via Instagram, if you must know), and I asked if she could share Darin's impact on her. Among many other beautiful things, she wrote:

"He has taught me to stop being so hard on myself as I have been a perfectionist my whole life. He allows me to be my true authentic self and accepts all my flaws, which he reminds me are not flaws but unique characteristics;)"

From an unrealistic idealist who snaps at everyone when they aren't reaching his expectations of perfection to a caring husband who encourages his wife to practice self-compassion—that's how Darin's ability to impact others has transformed! And it was only possible because he transformed his relationship with himself first.

You can't give what you don't have.

This is the thing to say back to your brain, over and over, when it tries to tell you that it's selfish to take care of your emotional fitness first, that you need to focus on others, that you're not a good leader or parent or friend if you don't put everyone's needs above yours. (I have this phrase invisibly tattooed on my forehead.)

If you're struggling and burning out daily, you can't improve the well-being of others or help them grow, and you can't do high-quality (or even decent-quality) work. I think you already know this intuitively.

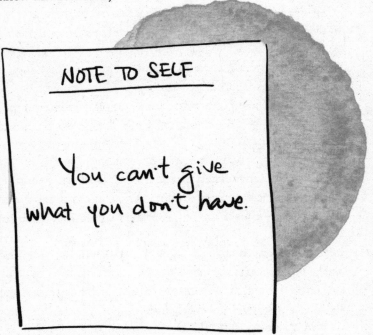

NOTE TO SELF

You can't give what you don't have.

But if you want some support, I've got it! Research shows that when you have greater well-being, you perform at your highest potential across every metric. You're more productive and creative, you make better decisions and are more likely to help others, you're more motivated to work through challenges, and you are more resilient as you get through them.

Doctors who report positive well-being make more accurate diagnoses.

Salespeople with greater well-being generate higher sales.

Leaders who are thriving have more people on their teams who thrive.

Parents who get some sleep don't snap at their children as much. (Okay, I didn't actually find research for this, but

I've got seventeen years of parenting experience to know this is true.)

We tend to think of our emotional fitness and well-being as separate from our work or caring for other people. But they're not—they're an essential part of our ability to do all of those things.

So please don't tell me you would love to be better at taking care of yourself but you need to take care of your work or other people first. Please don't tell me it's because "they need you!"

They don't need your overwhelm, exhaustion, or snapping at them because your fuse is on its shortest setting. What they need is your Awesome Human, fueled with energy, emotionally aware, and able to support them in meaningful ways.

LEADERSHIP

| Cultivate your own emotional fitness and well-being | Positively impact other people's capacity to thrive |

PRACTICE

Who and How Do I Want to Lead?

Use this practice to get specific about the impact you want to have on the people in your life, personally or through your work or craft.

Make two columns:

In the first, list the "who"—your family members, friends, team at work, colleagues, students, clients, other people you want to lead (Lead = positively impact their capacity to thrive).

In the second, list a few specific ways you want to positively impact them (e.g., *"I want to teach my daughter to treat herself with compassion so she isn't afraid of failure,"* or *"I want to fuel my team's confidence in their ability to get through the toughest challenges at work"*).

As you do this practice, think about how creating a more supportive relationship with yourself and strengthening your emotional fitness will help you impact others in the way that you'd like to.

Practice in This Chapter

Who and How Do I Want to Lead?

Your Note to Self

What is something you want to remember, practice, or reflect on from this chapter?

AWESOME HUMAN AWARD

I'm going to leave it up to you when to give yourself the Awesome Human Leadership award. This one might take a little time. I want you to actually embrace and begin to practice making your well-being and emotional fitness your number one responsibility so you can positively impact yourself and others. After you feel that you are, then go for it and give yourself the **Committed to Positively Impacting Other People's Capacity to Thrive** award!

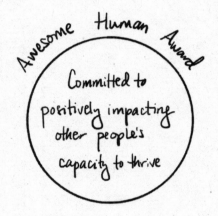

CHAPTER 8

Emotional Fitness Is Like Broccoli

Awesome Human Quality:
Commitment to Practicing Your Emotional Fitness Skills

Fair warning: if you hate broccoli, you won't enjoy the following analogy. But even if you're not a broccoli fan, you know it's good for you.

Here's the thing: just *knowing* that broccoli is good for you doesn't do you any good. Reading articles about the health benefits of broccoli is useless. Even having broccoli in your fridge does absolutely nothing.

You have to eat the broccoli to get the benefits of its vitamins and nutrients.

The same thing is true about emotional fitness.

Just reading about the importance of strengthening your emotional fitness or knowing that, yes, it's important, doesn't do you any good.

NOTE TO SELF

Emotional fitness
is a skill
you can improve
through practice.

You have to practice emotional fitness as a skill, consistently and regularly, to struggle less; have more energy; have a more supportive relationship with yourself, your thoughts, and your feelings; and positively impact other people.

I made this analogy earlier, but it's so good, I gotta bring it up again: think of emotional fitness as being like physical fitness but for your brain. To maintain your physical fitness, you need to work out and eat healthy food. And you need to do it consistently—you can't do it for a while and then be done with it. I mean, you can, but you'll be less fit.

To strengthen your emotional fitness, you need to commit to a regular practice of emotional fitness skills. Sure, after you practice for a while, you raise your baseline, but if you stop practicing you get rusty and your emotional fitness suffers.

There's no goal or final destination where you get to say, "Okay, I am done now!" Embracing your Awesome Human means making practicing emotional fitness skills and culti-vating a supportive relationship with yourself a regular part of your life and routine. For always.

Before you dive into your Five-Week Emotional Fitness Challenge, I want you to pause and get really clear about WHY you want to strengthen your emotional fitness.

There is no good why or bad why. There is only the true and meaningful WHY *for you*. And it doesn't need to be grand or world-saving. It just needs to be something that will remind you to practice, even when it's uncomfortable or your brain is trying to convince you not to do it.

To give you some inspirational fuel, here's how a few other Awesome Humans answered the question of why it was important to them to practice their emotional fitness skills:

> To feel a sense of freedom in a very busy and hectic life. To be a better parent, friend, wife, daughter, and sister.

> To feel more balanced and more energized instead of constantly dragging.

> To be able to be more present at home with my husband and kids.

> To be more authentic with my emotions and not always work so hard to hide my feelings behind a calm, collected face.

> To grow professionally and personally without constantly feeling overwhelmed.

> To feel as close to balanced as possible for a sustained period of time instead of going all out and then burning out.

Now it's your turn.

PRACTICE

Write Your Awesome Human Commitment

Write down your WHY for committing to practicing emotional fitness skills consistently and cultivating a more supportive relationship with yourself, your thoughts and emotions, and other people.

Think about these questions and jot down your answers:

How do you want to feel? (Be specific.)

Why is it important to you to feel this way?

Who, other than yourself, benefits when you feel this way? (E.g., colleagues, family, your work, your craft, etc.)

Next, write out your Awesome Human Commitment. Here's a format you might use:

"I am committed to embracing my Awesome Human by practicing emotional fitness skills and cultivating a more supportive relationship with myself because . . . (fill in with your WHY)."

You can use whatever format you want! The only thing I ask is that you use words that mean something to you. Don't worry about how it sounds—no one else has to read it. This is your commitment to *yourself.*

Keep your Awesome Human Commitment somewhere you can see it often. You could even take a photo of it so you can glance at it on your phone (because you know you're doing a lot of glancing at your phone!).

Practice in This Chapter
Write Your Awesome Human Commitment

Your Note to Self
What is something you want to remember, practice, or reflect on from this chapter?

AWESOME HUMAN AWARD

After you've written your Awesome Human Commitment and are ready to begin your Five-Week Emotional Fitness Challenge, give yourself the **Awesome Human-in-Training** award! You've already practiced a LOT of essential skills to improve your relationship with yourself, your thoughts, and your emotions, and you are well on your way to embracing your Awesome Human!

PART III

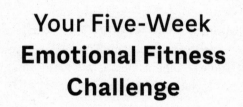

Your Five-Week
Emotional Fitness
Challenge

You're here! I'm so excited to welcome you to your Five-Week Emotional Fitness Challenge. For the next five weeks, you're going to learn and practice the five emotional fitness skills.

5 Emotional Fitness Skills

Acceptance — Gratitude — Self-care — Intentional kindness — Bigger Why

Here are a few guiding principles for your challenge:

- **Focus on one skill per week.** You'll be able to make more progress this way, and that will help your brain feel more confident about learning the other skills, some of which might be more challenging than others.

- **Focus on one skill, but don't lose the others.** Use the 80/20 rule: give 80 percent of your attention to the focus skill for each week and 20 percent to the previous skills.

- **Practice daily.** It's easier to stick to doing something if you do it every day, especially when you're building new habits. So I'm asking you to practice daily throughout your challenge. (You'll have a focus practice for each skill and a few others to choose from.)

- **There's no such thing as "falling off the wagon."** Seriously, there isn't. If you only get to do one practice in a given week or have to pause your project for a week or two because work is crazy or you have stuff going on at home, that's okay. Just pick up where you left off.

- **Practice in every part of your life.** To get the most out of your Awesome Human Project, I encourage you to practice these emotional fitness skills in every part of your life—on your own, in your relationships, with friends and people you don't know, at work and outside of work. You'll find that when you challenge yourself to practice these skills in situations that feel most uncomfortable, you'll often experience the biggest and most unexpected benefits.

- **Use your Awesome Human Qualities.** You'll need to practice courage, self-compassion, emotional awareness and openness, leadership, and commitment to go through this challenge. You might find it helpful to refer back to part I from time to time to refresh your memory and maybe even do some of the practices to strengthen your Awesome Human Qualities.

- **Don't take yourself too seriously.** Give yourself some space to have fun with this challenge, to smile, and to kindly laugh at yourself and your brain when it tries to steer you sideways. Ram Dass, one of the most well-known spiritual teachers who has greatly influenced me and my work, has a wonderful quote that I offer to you as you launch into your Five-Week Emotional Fitness Challenge:

"Either you do it like it's a big weight on you, or you do it as part of the dance."
Let's dance!

CHAPTER 9

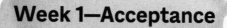

Week 1—Acceptance

This week you're going to be practicing the skill of Acceptance, and I want to be honest with you: this might be the toughest emotional fitness skill to master. But the good news is that you've already begun to practice it, even if you didn't know what it was called.

Acceptance is the skill of acknowledging the situation and your feelings with clarity instead of getting caught up in the story your brain has created and using that as your starting point to decide the best way forward. Every time you edit your story and your thoughts and witness yourself instead of judging yourself, you're practicing Acceptance. So you see, I'm not making you start with the toughest skill without giving you some practice first!

I used to hate the word *acceptance*! It felt like resignation or rolling over and just accepting everything as it was without trying to solve problems or make things better. I hated that!

Coming to the United States as a refugee when I was a teenager was such a difficult experience that it cemented my view of life as a fight: me against tough reality. I fully embraced my identity as a fighter, fixer, and improver! If there was a problem, or something wasn't how I thought it should have been—at work, in my family—I felt an immediate sense of responsibility to jump in and try to change it. When friends or colleagues shared something they were struggling with, I would immediately go into fixer mode, flooding them with advice whether they asked for it or not. I was also a devoted people improver, always on the lookout for how I could "help" people I cared about get better, which often meant pestering them with endless advice and suggestions.

I constantly found things in my life that weren't as I thought they should have been—including myself—and I tried to change them. And if I couldn't change them, I would waste so much energy beating myself up for not being good enough or feeling frustrated at a world clearly against me. I would get stuck in the Valley of Struggle, the space between how something was and how my brain had decided it *should* have been.

The idea that some things were outside of my control wasn't something I was ever willing to consider.

In 2008, smack in the middle of the housing and financial crisis, I was running a startup I'd founded, a community for working moms called *Work It, Mom.* We'd raised some money from angel investors to get it going and needed to raise another round of capital. But as hard as I tried, in the end, we couldn't raise the money we needed and had to sell the company at a loss.

I was absolutely devastated. I'd failed our angel investors, people who worked with me, thousands of moms in our community, and my own dream of starting and growing a company. I was certain the *only* reason we didn't succeed was because I wasn't good enough as the CEO. And that crushed me.

I was pouring out some of my self-criticism to Adam, a good friend who had a lot of experience with startups. At one point he interrupted me: "So, let me get this straight: you couldn't raise venture capital for a startup that relies on advertising revenue in the midst of the worst economic crisis in the last decade, when huge companies were going bankrupt and the economy is collapsing. And you don't think *any* other factors could have contributed to your failure to raise capital other than your inadequacy?!"

Adam was trying to get me to acknowledge that I was doing something really difficult (fewer than 1 percent of startups raise venture money) during a really difficult time (one of the worst recessions in history) and to accept that many factors might have contributed to my inability to succeed. But I didn't want to hear it. Those were just excuses, in my mind. There were founders who had raised capital during that time, and I wasn't one of them, so who cares how difficult it was—the failure was obviously 100 percent my fault.

I was completely attached to the story my brain had told me: I *should* have been able to raise capital, and I didn't because I was an incompetent entrepreneur. And I spent months stuck in the Valley of Struggle, pummeling myself with harsh self-criticism and crumbling from feeling like a complete failure. I swore off ever starting a company or joining a startup again and ended up taking a job at a large company in a role that didn't excite me or use any of my skills or strengths (I hated it!).

I wasted so much energy, caused myself and people around me so much emotional pain, and made a decision I ended up regretting because I couldn't bring myself to accept reality: raising money during an economic collapse was very difficult, and I hadn't been able to do it. It didn't make me a failure or a horrible entrepreneur. It just meant that I couldn't raise money for my company at that time.

Acceptance doesn't have anything to do with resignation, giving up, or being passive. Just like self-acceptance, Acceptance is the skill of boldly embracing reality so you can stop wasting energy fighting it and instead use that energy to figure out the best way forward given how things are and how you feel.

From Should to Could

Acceptance is made up of two distinct steps.

Step 1: Acknowledge the situation and your feelings with clarity instead of getting caught up in the story your brain is telling you.

Remember, clarity is all about the facts: what do you *know* to be true?

Let's go back to our favorite Tense Boss scenario and see how this step might work in practice:

Story	Fact
"My boss should be smiling because she always smiles when we meet!"	"My boss isn't smiling."
"My boss is not smiling, so she must be upset with me!"	"My boss is not smiling."
"My boss seems tense, so that means I'm about to get bad feedback."	"My boss seems tense."

If this seems familiar, it should be. We talked about the difference between witnessing yourself (facts) versus judging yourself (stories) in chapter 5, on self-compassion. Judgments and stories always imply some kind of a deterministic conclusion—here is *why* my boss isn't smiling—whereas the facts are just that, facts—my boss isn't smiling.

Because your boss usually smiles in meetings, your brain decided that was how it *should* always be. So when she didn't smile in this particular meeting, your brain immediately dragged you into the Valley of Struggle: *My boss should be smiling, and she is not because I suck at my job, and she is about to fire me.* A lot of struggle and wasted energy!

But using the first step of Acceptance, you can course correct your brain's stress-inducing storytelling and just focus on the facts: *My boss isn't smiling and seems tense.* Now, instead of wasting all that energy on worst-case scenarios, you get to decide how best to move forward.

You can shift from should to could.

This is what the second step of Acceptance helps you to do:

Step 2: Given the facts, identify one thing you could do to move forward.

Notice how this step doesn't say, "Make everything better and amazing so that it's exactly 100 percent how you wish it were!"

Just identify one step you *could* take to move forward in a way that reduces your struggle and serves you, the situation, and anyone else involved in the best way you can think of.

What might that step be in our imaginary meeting?

Well, it seems like a good idea to ask your boss how she is doing and if everything is okay.

So, let's say you go ahead and ask: "Is everything okay? You seem a bit stressed today."

How might your boss respond?

"Oh, thanks for asking," she says. "I just came out of a really stressful meeting with our product vice president. Apparently, the product team feels we're not collaborating and sharing enough info with them, and let's just say he didn't use the kindest words to relay this to me."

Drumroll, please:

You don't suck at your job, and YOU ARE NOT GETTING FIRED!!!

Your boss is tense because she just had a stressful meeting. She doesn't hate your work. Or you. This is not about you at all!

Now, of course there is a chance that your boss's answer confirms your suspicions, and it turns out she is, in fact, unhappy about something you've done. I'm not suggesting that it would be pleasant to hear that. But it is better not to *assume* that's the case because making that assumption causes you to struggle.

This is a really important point because it connects to so much of what you're learning and practicing during your Awesome Human Project:

You can't choose when and how challenges, difficulties, or situations you wish were different come your way. But you *can choose how much you struggle* when they do come and how you spend your energy.

When your boss doesn't smile during a meeting—a situation you wish were different—you can choose to increase your struggle by letting your brain make up all kinds of worst-case scenarios or you can choose to reduce your struggle by not making those assumptions, focusing on the facts, and then taking the best step to move forward (asking your boss if everything is okay). When you struggle less, you have more energy and capacity to actually do something to help you work through the challenge; when you struggle more, you have less energy.

Recognizing that you have the choice to struggle less is liberating, but it's also daunting. To make it, you need to change your familiar thought patterns and edit the stories your brain makes up, which are often convincing. This is HARD to do, especially at the beginning. I respect you too much to pretend otherwise.

But it is a choice you can always make, and the only question you need to answer is:

Do I want to struggle less or more?

By the way, if it turns out that yes, your boss is unhappy with your performance, you get to choose what to do given that reality. After you know the facts, you can think of what you *could* do, which is way more productive than wasting your energy being upset that your reality is not the way it *should* be.

This shift from *should* to *could* is really powerful.

Should feels like a trap; it takes away your power and creates tension between you and reality. Think of how you feel when you think: *These people are not acting the way they should!* or *I should be doing better than I am! Should* is shorthand for judgment and struggle.

Could opens up possibilities. It empowers you to make choices about what to do and helps you to feel a sense of control. Notice the difference: *This person seems upset. What's the best thing I could do?* or *What could I do to improve? Could* is shorthand for choice and possibility.

The shift from *should* to *could* is the biggest gift of Acceptance, and I'm so excited for you to start practicing this skill!

Your focus practice for the week is the **Lens of Acceptance.**

A physical lens focuses light. We have lenses in our eyes that help us focus light so we can see, and when they don't work well, we wear glasses or contact lenses to help us see better. In the same way, a mental lens helps you to intentionally focus your attention. I really love this concept, and your focus practice for each emotional fitness skill during the Five-Week Emotional Fitness Challenge is a lens through which you'll practice focusing your attention.

You get to choose your mental lens

PRACTICE

Lens of Acceptance

Do this practice when you recognize that your brain is dragging you into the Valley of Struggle and you're getting frustrated that something is not as it should be. (This is a GREAT practice to do right after Struggle Awareness.)

Step 1: Acknowledge a difficult situation and your feelings about it with clarity instead of judgment.

Ask: *What are the facts I know to be true right now?*

Witness versus judge.

Focus on the present moment versus everything that led up to it.

Remember that facts are what you know to be true.

Check in with yourself to become aware of your feelings (without judgment)—acknowledging your feelings is an important part of this step.

Step 2: Identify one specific step you could take to move forward right now.

Ask: *What is one thing I could do right now to help myself struggle less and move forward in the best way?*

This can be a really small step, but it helps to shift your brain's attention to doing something helpful and productive.

Taking one step will lead you to think of more because your brain loves a sense of progress!

Here are some examples of how the Lens of Acceptance helps you see your way out of the Valley of Struggle:

Valley of Struggle	Acceptance
"The weather is awful! It shouldn't be raining this hard right now, and it's ruining our vacation!"	"It's raining, and it's frustrating that it's happening while we're on vacation. But we could go to the movies or bowling and still have fun together!"
"The client hasn't called back in a week. It definitely means we didn't get the deal and this year will be awful for the business!"	"We haven't heard from the client in a week, which is unusual for them. I could send an email to check in—maybe our contact is dealing with something personally."
"We spent an hour waiting in line, and now they say they don't have the car we reserved! They should have told us earlier or had more cars!"	"They don't have the car we reserved, and I'm stressed out. We don't want to waste more time, so we could just take whatever option they do have."
"Ugh! My colleague didn't finish her part of the presentation and now we're behind. She should have told us earlier!"	"Our presentation will be late, and I'm annoyed. I'll let our boss know we need an extra day."
"I should have done better in that interview but I screwed up, and now I'll never get a job I want."	"That was a stressful interview, and I could have done better. I'm going to bust my butt preparing for the next one."

The thing I want you to hear loud and clear about Acceptance is that no one is asking you to like the challenge or problem you're facing. Not at all! There are many times when life sucks or things are not going the way you wish they were. But what I *am* asking you to do is not to waste your limited emotional and mental energy being stuck in the Valley of Struggle so that you can use that energy to figure how to move forward.

Please Stop Shoulding Yourself (It Will Help You Feel Less Overwhelmed)

One of the ways we cause ourselves so much more struggle is by constantly "shoulding" ourselves. How often does your brain say something like:

I should be more organized.

I should lose weight.

I should call my friend.

I should be further along in my career.

I should spend less time on my phone.

I want you to pause and think about how it *feels* when you get into the "should." For me, "should" feels like resistance, like I am failing at something and starting from behind. This is another version of the Valley of Struggle: I get stuck in the space between how I am and how my brain has decided I *should* be. It feels draining, demoralizing, and deflating—and starting from the "should" definitely doesn't inspire me to do the thing my brain is shoulding me to do!

A few days ago, I had a chance to talk with a woman named Rocio. She reached out for some encouragement and advice

NOTE TO SELF

Don't should yourself!

about how to move forward after a year where nothing was as it should have been. She had lost her job suddenly. Her beloved father had passed away. And after years of dealing with a debilitating illness, she had surgery, which left her in recovery mode and unable to look for a new job for six months.

That's a lot for anyone to handle, and Rocio told me she was stuck. She knew she "should" be getting out there and looking for a new job, especially because her health insurance was running out and she needed new coverage. "But when I think about all the things I should do, I just get so overwhelmed that I don't even start," she told me.

I asked Rocio to become the editor of her thoughts and shift from "should" to "could." Instead of thinking about all the things she should do over the next several months to get a new job, could she identify a few specific small things she could do today and tomorrow? "What is one thing you could do to begin?" I asked her.

NOTE TO SELF

Instead of wasting your energy worrying about how you will get it done, start doing.

Joan Miró is one of my favorite abstract artists. I once read an interview where he talked about painting like a gardener. He said that he would often draw a line on a canvas, and then leave it there for a few days. Then he would come back and add another shape, and then another, and like a gardener, he would tend to this growing painting over time, each new element inspiring the next.

I love this analogy, and I shared it with Rocio. "Start with one line on your canvas and then see where it leads you. Don't try to figure out the whole painting—a.k.a. all the things about your new job and how you will get it—just start with one action, one line, and then see what next step it invites. Keep going that way, keep thinking, 'What is the next thing I could do? What is the next shape I want to draw on my canvas?'"

Rocio's face became less tense as we talked, and she was excited to start taking steps and being the gardener of her next job. She told me she felt there was so much within her, but she was holding it back, and maybe this was a way she could begin to remove the layers. I loved witnessing her begin to embrace her Awesome Human and share more of her with the world.

When you get stuck in the Valley of Struggle of the "should" or feel overwhelmed with thoughts of all the things you need to do, I encourage you to think of this analogy of a gardener or painter. Instead of thinking of the big goal you're aiming for, staying trapped in the thoughts of all the things you should have done in the past or all the things you should be doing, begin by drawing one line on your canvas. Identify one specific thing you can do right now, one small step you can take forward. Then identify another. Keep taking steps, one at a time, and when your brain wants to drag you into the Valley of Struggle, use your Lens of Acceptance to bring it back to this moment: *Given how things are, what is the next best thing I could do?*

Here are a few examples of what shifting from "should" to "could" looks like:

Should	Could
"I should be more organized."	"I could organize my desk later today."
"I should lose weight."	"I could start by skipping sugar in my coffee."
"I should call my friend."	"I could call my friend while I'm out for my walk this evening."
"I should be further along in my career."	"I could look into taking some leadership courses to get ready for my next career move."
"I should spend less time on my phone."	"I could put away my phone after 9 p.m."

How to Stop Wasting Energy Assuming What Others Expect of You

Just as your brain loves to make up stories about what other people think or why they do what they do, it also loves to make up assumptions about what other people expect of you.

Ami is a friend who was a member of our Elevating Women Leaders program. Around Christmas last year, she texted me to ask if I would help her get out of the Valley of Struggle. She was super-frustrated because instead of enjoying her time off work with her family at home, she was feeling sick and had an annoying cough that kept her up at night.

"This is not how holiday time should be! It should be fun and relaxing," Ami told me.

We walked through the two steps of the Lens of Acceptance together. Ami acknowledged she couldn't magically make her body *not* feel sick, and maybe this was a sign that she needed to slow down and try to do less on her vacation, not more. But as we chatted, it became clear that something else was keeping Ami in the Valley of Struggle:

"I'm always the one organizing all the celebrations and being cheerful, and now I can't even do that! I feel like I'm disappointing my son and my husband," she said.

There it was: Ami had *assumed* that her son and husband expected her to be the energizer bunny of cheer, and she was sad to disappoint them.

So I asked if she would consider telling her family about how she felt. What would happen if she came clean about her disappointment over not being able to be her usual holiday organizer self?

Ami agreed to give it a shot, and a few days later, she texted me an adorable picture of her son holding a "Get well!" sign he had painted for her. She said that acknowledging how she felt to her family was really helpful, and they actually did some things they hadn't done before to bring cheer to the holiday season.

Practicing Acceptance not only helped Ami get out of the Valley of Struggle but it also gave her an opening not to pressure herself into being the perfect cheerleader mom and wife around the holidays—and gave her son and her husband an opportunity to step in and help!

There's a lesson here for all of us: **practicing Acceptance out loud can often lead to wonderfully unexpected outcomes, including making your relationships with other people more honest and open.**

When, instead of assuming you know what people expect from you, you tell them how you feel, you give *them* an opportunity to tell you how *they feel.* Your opening up is an act of respect and humility. Instead of acting like you're some all-knowing guru, you accept that you might not know what the other person feels or thinks.

So often, when you share your worry about disappointing someone, you learn that the fear was unfounded or exaggerated. Or you give yourself and the other people an opportunity to create more helpful "rules of engagement" for everyone involved. By always taking on the responsibility of being the upbeat energy center of her family, Ami actually didn't allow her son and her husband to step in and help. They assumed that this is how things were and perhaps that Ami wanted it to be that way.

If you're always jumping in to do something—take notes in a meeting, say yes to a colleague's request, make dinner, and so forth—other people will assume that's what you want to keep doing. So they'll let you keep doing it, which will lead you to assume that's what they expect of you. And boom, you're stuck in the Valley of Struggle, feeling overcommitted and resentful that others aren't jumping in to help.

My husband told me that his fourth-grade teacher used to say, "Assuming is making an ass of you and me." I love that. Don't make an ass of yourself and other people by getting stuck in the Valley of Struggle of assumptions. Honor their humanity and your own by practicing your Acceptance openly and giving everyone a chance to share how they really feel and think. This might not be easy to do, but I promise you it will lead you out of the Valley of Struggle.

What to Do When There's Nothing You "Could" Do (a.k.a. How to Accept Difficult Feelings)

Sometimes when you practice the first step of Acceptance, you realize there is nothing you can do about a situation you're facing. There isn't a "could" that can help you move forward. But this isn't an excuse to slip into the Valley of Struggle—it's an invitation to practice accepting your difficult feelings about the situation.

My daughter, Mia, taught me a powerful lesson about this a few years ago. She was in eighth grade, and on the students' end-of-year trip to Montreal, the girls she had been friends with decided to pull that middle-school mean-girl stunt and kick her out of their friend circle.

Here she was, away from home and facing something incredibly difficult and heartbreaking. (If you've gone through something like this, you know it's a gut punch. If you've been a parent of a child going through this, you know it hits you even harder.)

A few weeks after this happened, Mia's English teacher gave the students an assignment to write their version of the middle-school graduation speech. Mia's speech was one of the biggest gifts I've gotten as a mom: it was about how Acceptance helped her survive middle school, especially the incident with her friends.

She wrote about how after it happened, she was consumed with thoughts of what she might have done to cause her friends to reject her. But after a while, she realized that it had nothing to do with what she did and, more importantly, that there was nothing she *could* do to change the situation. Her friendship with this group of friends was over, and instead of ruminating on why or struggling with it, she needed to accept what had happened.

I know this wasn't easy for her. It's not easy for any of us to feel rejected or to face a difficult situation we can't change or control, including the actions of other people, which might be causing us pain, sadness, frustration, or stress. But here, again, we have a choice: to get stuck in the *"this is not how it should be"* Valley of Struggle or to practice accepting our feelings about the situation, however difficult they might be.

So, how do you accept difficult feelings?

This answer might annoy you: you accept your difficult feelings by feeling them.

The only way to the other side of a difficult feeling is through fully embracing it.

Sounds good, but what the heck does it actually mean to embrace your difficult feelings?

First, and most importantly, DON'T JUDGE YOUR FEELINGS! Our brains are so good at judging our feelings and making us feel even worse that I feel compelled to use all caps for emphasis.

You: *I feel stressed.*

Brain: *It's Sunday, and it's sunny out, and you feel stressed? That's just wrong. You should not feel stressed on a sunny weekend day!*

You: *I feel nervous.*

Brain: *You're pathetic to feel nervous. If you were better at this, you wouldn't feel nervous. You're weak to feel nervous.*

Ugh! The only outcome of judging your feelings is that you feel worse.

But there is no "should" when it comes to your feelings! You're a human being, not a machine. Your feelings don't have a schedule; they don't know when it's the weekend or when you're about to go on vacation. They show up when they show up.

Instead of letting your brain judge your feelings, help it to see them through the Lens of Acceptance:

You: *I feel stressed.*

Brain: *It's Sunday, and it's sunny out, and you feel stressed? That's just wrong. You should not feel stressed on a sunny weekend day!*

You: *Okay, stop! This is not helpful at all. Feelings are feelings. Instead of judging, how about coming up with something I could do to feel a little better?*

Brain: *Okay . . . how about you take a short walk outside? Fresh air usually gives you a boost.*

You: *A walk sounds good, actually!*

By practicing Acceptance, you've reduced struggle. Instead of feeling bad about your emotions, you've given yourself permission to feel them, and that helped you to identify something you *could* do to try to feel a little bit better. This might not seem like a big deal, but it is.

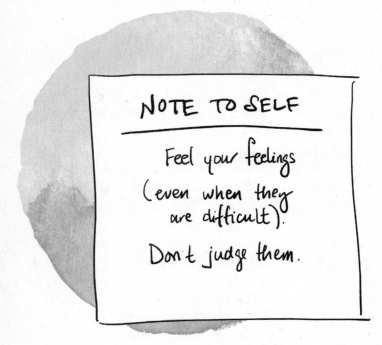

NOTE TO SELF

Feel your feelings (even when they are difficult).

Don't judge them.

Research shows that when we do something to reduce our stress, it matters less what it is and more that we're choosing to do it. If you believe that eating twenty-five almonds or making paper airplanes will reduce your stress, it will! This is actually how placebos work: some studies have shown that even when people know they are being given a placebo, if they believe it will have its intended effect, they are likely to experience it.

So just making the decision to accept your feelings and do something to help yourself feel a little better actually helps you. But I want to share a few more specific tips to help you practice accepting difficult and uncomfortable feelings, just in case eating almonds or making paper airplanes isn't your thing:

- **Name your feeling.** Be specific, and name your feelings out loud to yourself if you can.

  "I feel sad that my friend hasn't called me" is better than "I feel sad," and "I feel worried about getting this job" is better than "I feel worried" because when you are specific, it's easier to come up with something you can do to feel a little better.

- **Add "right now' to how you feel.** Instead of saying "I feel sad," say "I feel sad *right now.*"

  Reminding yourself that your feelings are temporary helps you to experience them with a little more ease.

- **Remember that you can feel more than one emotion at a time.** Become aware of and name other feelings you're experiencing, which will help your difficult feeling become less dominant (and easier to feel).

  Recognize that you have the capacity to experience many seemingly conflicting emotions at the same time. You can feel sadness *and* joy, hope *and* worry, stress *and* a sense of purpose.

- **Practice self-compassion (a.k.a. treat yourself as a friend).** Imagine a good friend is experiencing the same difficult feelings: how would you support him?

   What supportive words might you say? Say those words to yourself.

- **Do something that brings you comfort.** Ask yourself what would feel comforting right now and do it: have a cup of tea, take a walk, watch a fun show.

   Do this as a way to care of yourself rather than to avoid feeling your feelings.

My last piece of advice about difficult feelings might sound ridiculous and counterintuitive:

Don't half-ass your difficult feelings! When you feel something, however difficult, the best thing you can do is allow yourself to feel all the way. The sooner you can do that, the less resistance you create between you and your feelings and the easier your path through them.

If you're worried, worry. Do it as an activity: *I'm going to worry right now.* Don't let your worried thoughts run on an endless loop in the background. Acknowledge what you feel, name the feeling, and get specific about your worry. Doing this helps to calm your brain, and it's like talking to small children having a tantrum: you want to let them know that you care, that you're there with them, and that you'd like to learn about what upset them.

So here's a practice to help you not half-ass your difficult feelings. I picked stress because it's something we all feel way too often, but you can use this practice for any difficult emotion this week.

PRACTICE

Embrace Your Stress

Give yourself five to ten minutes to feel what you feel. (You might want to set a timer.) Tell your brain that this is your time to stress out—no judgment.

Take out a piece of paper (if you're on the go, you can always use the Notes app on your phone) and write about your stress. Don't judge—just write down everything you're stressed out about.

When your five to ten minutes are up, read through what you wrote. Is there anything you can learn? Does one item jump out as THE thing that's causing most of your stress, and could you do something about it? Has your brain made up negative and dramatic stories you could edit?

Sometimes there's nothing to learn, and this practice gives you a chance to simply acknowledge your stress. Great! Remember that when you name your feelings, you feel them with less intensity and for a shorter period.

After you're done, take a deep breath and give yourself permission to move on with your day. Your brain will have an easier time letting you do it because you've acknowledged how it feels.

AWESOME HUMAN AWARD

Accepting your difficult feelings instead of judging yourself for having them is a big step. So after you've practiced doing this a few times, definitely give yourself the **No More "Shoulding" Myself** award. You've earned it, and it will be a great reminder to keep practicing!

Don't Make Your Difficult Feelings Worse by Telling Dramatic Stories about Them

There is a difference between feeling your difficult and uncomfortable feelings and getting wrapped up in stories your brain creates about them.

Let's say you're having a tough day—totally normal. You're a human being, and part of the deal is that sometimes we have bad days. But don't make your bad day worse by telling yourself a story about how bad it is and how much you hate it and how much it sucks and on and on. When you get too attached to the story of how bad your day is, you rob yourself of the little uplifting moments of goodness, kindness, warmth, or just okay-ness that might sneak into it. And these moments can become your source of strength and energy to help you get through your tough day.

NOTE TO SELF

The story you tell yourself about your day impacts how you feel.

Edit your story.

The mental model you choose for your day determines how you feel throughout the day because, remember, your brain sees things not as they are but as it believes they are. So if your mental model is "This is a horrible day!" your brain will constantly look for proof that, yes, it's a horrible day! It will flex its negativity bias muscle and make sure you notice every single situation that could make you feel more upset and ignore anything positive that doesn't fit into the horrible day framework.

I wrote about the difference between feeling difficult emotions and telling stories about them in my weekly Happier email and got this email back from Ariane:

> This is exactly what I've been going through for three months: telling myself over and over again "I'm not OK, I'm really not OK, I'm exhausted, everyone at work thinks I'm annoying, I'm bad at my job, I just want to go to sleep.... And then, your email arrived!
>
> And I realized a couple of things: By telling myself this story, I wasn't giving myself space to feel or think anything else! Joy,

hope, anything really. I was SO determined not to be OK that when I actually was OK, I wasn't accepting it! I was just counting the days and hours before my next down.

That impacted me, my self-esteem, my work, but also everyone around me. I was becoming the "sad, stressed, not OK girl" because I didn't let myself have space to be anything else and to let my colleagues see the happy, joyful, active part of me. So THANK YOU for this "Aha moment!"

This! I love the clarity with which Ariane's email speaks to the fact that accepting your difficult feelings doesn't mean rejecting all other feelings.

Feel what you feel, but don't keep telling yourself a story about it. And if you feel something different, even for a bit, allow yourself to feel that, too!

Acceptance Also Means Accepting Other People's Difficult Feelings

In my experience, the only thing harder than making peace with our own difficult feelings is allowing people we care about to feel theirs.

When my daughter is sad, I want to do anything humanly possible to help her not feel that way. I love her bajillions, and even though I know sadness is part of life, I want her to feel better. It's painful to see people we love struggle, and it's completely natural to want to help them feel better or cheer them up.

This desire comes from love . . . but it also comes from our own discomfort around other people's difficult feelings. When my daughter feels upset, it's difficult for me to let her feel those feelings. It's uncomfortable, and often I feel helpless and like there is something I "should" be doing to fix it.

So this is where my own practice of Acceptance comes in. I'm not going to pretend that I'm amazing at this 100 percent of the time, but learning how to accept that, yes, sometimes Mia feels sad or upset and that's okay—and it's also okay that as her mom, this is difficult and uncomfortable for me to experience—has been powerful. She and I both have more space for our feelings, and our relationship with each other is more honest because she doesn't feel the need to pretend to be great all the time. And the thing I learn over and over is that when I don't jump in to try to immediately improve how my daughter feels but instead validate her feelings and simply let her know that I'm here if she needs anything, she gets through them a little easier, on her own.

Validating someone's feelings doesn't mean you want the person to feel them or you agree with them. You're simply saying, *I understand that this is how you feel, and I don't need you to change how you feel right now.* If this seems too passive or as if you're not doing enough to help, I want to assure you that you are. We so often underestimate the value of our presence, care, and attention. But especially when others are struggling, these are the most valuable gifts you can offer them. Knowing that we're not alone is one of our core human needs, and as you'll learn in chapter 12, during your week of Intentional Kindness, just feeling connected to others helps us to feel a little (or a lot) better.

So this is your advanced Acceptance practice when someone you care about is struggling: to validate their feelings and allow them not to be okay.

I also encourage you to ask the person how you could help when they feel stressed or upset. Mia actually taught me this lesson, and I love that! I roped her into making a few YouTube videos with me to share advice with teens and their parents, and we made one about how to help your kids when they are upset. In the video, Mia said, "Don't be afraid to ask what your kids want you to do when they feel down! Like, I like to be left alone for a while, but I also love when my mom brings me snacks." (Snacks are totally part of my love language!)

Ask the people you care about how you can help when they feel down. Do they want to be left alone? Cheered up? Do they want snacks or silly gifs? Do they want to vent or be distracted? You're an Awesome Human, not a mind reader, so go ahead and ask. They will love that you did!

Enthusiastic Acceptance (or, Your Graduate-Level Acceptance Practice)

Acceptance is one of the toughest skills to master, but I'm so confident in you that I'm going to throw one more practice at you this week. I call it Enthusiastic Acceptance.

Here's the idea behind it: when something unpleasant, unexpected, or frustrating happens, can you see it as an invitation to do something new and different, to literally grow and expand in new and different ways?

This came up in my recent conversation with Diana, one of the awesome women leaders I work with. Her boss and mentor had left somewhat unexpectedly, and her replacement had a very different leadership style that was a challenge for Diana. At the same time, the company shifted priorities, and the project she and her team had worked on for a year was put on hold. Understandably, she was feeling lost.

So I asked her to practice Enthusiastic Acceptance: What if she imagined that everything that happened was exactly as it should be? Could she see this as an awesome opportunity, an invitation to grow in new ways—in her career, as a leader, within the company?

Immediately, Diana shifted from being stuck in frustration to coming up with ideas and thinking of different possibilities. She emailed me a few months later and, with excitement, shared some of the new career opportunities she was considering. Practicing Enthusiastic Acceptance helped her see a challenging situation from a completely different perspective, which allowed her to take steps she wouldn't have considered otherwise.

I encourage you to use this practice to approach a challenge you're dealing with this week, but you can always keep it in your arsenal for when life throws a serious curveball your way.

PRACTICE

Enthusiastic Acceptance

When something unexpected, frustrating, or challenging happens, consider for a moment that this is exactly what should be happening. I know this might seem odd, and your brain will definitely argue, and please remember I am not asking you to like the situation. Just imagine it this way to help shift your perspective.

Then, ask yourself:

What is this situation inviting me to do that I might not have considered otherwise?

How can I use this opportunity to do something that helps me grow or improve in a way that's meaningful to me?

What would I do if I were really excited about this situation?

I encourage you not to get caught up in the details but to use this practice to help you imagine possibilities you might not have considered before.

I want to leave you with one more thought about Acceptance that I find really helpful, especially when my brain is stubborn about keeping me in the Valley of Struggle:

Any little shift you can make from "this is not how it should be" to "this is one thing I could do to move forward" is a big deal. That one step out of the Valley of Struggle helps you use your energy productively and sets you on a path of possibility, finding more and more steps to take. So really, it can never be too small!

Practices in This Chapter

Lens of Acceptance
Embrace Your Stress
Enthusiastic Acceptance

Your Note to Self

What is something you want to remember, practice, or reflect on from this chapter?

AWESOME HUMAN AWARD

After you've done your practices for the week, you're ready for your **Climbed Out of the Valley of Struggle!** award. I want you to feel really proud of this one—keeping yourself and your brain out of the Valley of Struggle is definitely a challenge!

CHAPTER 10

Week 2—Gratitude

This week you're going to become a Gratitude Hero by kickstarting your Gratitude habit (or strengthening one you already have). And because last week I told you that Acceptance would be the toughest emotional fitness skill to master, let me start with some good news: you're about to have a really great week.

I'm willing to promise you this even though I don't know what might be going on in your life. As long as you commit to practicing Gratitude daily, my promise stands. No other skill takes the steam out of your brain's negativity bias and helps to uplift you, even on the toughest days, the way Gratitude does.

Gratitude is the skill of actively appreciating the small, positive moments in everyday life—even when times are challenging—and sharing your appreciation for other people with them.

Before we dive in, a confession: I used to think that Gratitude was cheesy and a bunch of BS.

When I first came to the United States, I thought Gratitude was that thing you did on Thanksgiving, where you went around the table, said thanks for the food and your friends and

The Awesome Human Project

family, and then gobbled up the food (OMG, so much food—I love Thanksgiving!).

Doing this once a year seemed just fine. But when I was really struggling, I came across research suggesting Gratitude was something I should practice regularly, not just on the day when I eat too much turkey. There are something like eleven thousand different studies showing that Gratitude is one of the most effective ways to boost your mood, reduce stress, and even improve sleep. I read a lot of this research, and it seemed convincing, but I didn't want to be convinced. Gratitude felt very "woo-woo," and my brain kept telling me that it was like putting on rose-colored glasses and pretending that everything was great when it wasn't.

But the real reason I was a Gratitude skeptic was because it threatened my lifelong commitment to the story that struggle was the only path to happiness. I believed that you must struggle to achieve and accomplish big things and doing that is what *earned* you the right to feel joy, happiness, contentment, and a sense of peace. I was a staunch proponent of the *I'll be happy when . . .* philosophy: *I'll be happy when I've achieved all the things I want to achieve; taken care of everyone I care about; and oh, become the ultimate perfect version I have in mind for myself.* Then and only then would I feel that I had earned the right to feel good.

So the idea that I could practice Gratitude and feel good right then and there, in the present moment, *before* I'd checked all the achievements and struggles off my list, was both threatening to the story I'd believed for so long and a bit ridiculous. Still, I decided to give Gratitude a try, mostly because I felt desperate to feel a little better (even though I thought I couldn't).

I found a way to allow my stubborn brain to give me permission to do it: I did it as an experiment, which meant I didn't need to drop my struggle story. During my Thirty-Day Gratitude Experiment, I committed to writing down three

162

good things about my day and having one kind and grateful interaction with another person. I was certain I would get through my experiment, the "woo-woo" of gratitude would fail to work for me, and then I could comfortably stay where I was: struggling but proud to have proven 11,000 studies wrong. The possibility of proving all this research wrong made my brain *very* excited.

You can guess the punch line: my brain had to admit defeat (reluctantly). Even against all of my inner resistance, Gratitude worked for me just like the research said it would. It wasn't some huge magical fix that made me feel amazing—not at all. But for what felt like the first time in my life, I was *enjoying* the simplest everyday moments without running through them on autopilot. I'm talking about really small things, like sitting down with a cup of coffee, having a quick chat with my daughter before work, or pausing to look at the tulips on our kitchen counter because they looked beautiful in the sunlight.

I won't lie, it felt awkward and sometimes silly to sit down and write my three Gratitude moments for the day. My brain was at the ready to sabotage my practice and convince me that I was being absolutely ridiculous to think small things like this mattered when there were huge problems in my life that really needed my attention. I often felt like I was cheating on reality by finding these little joys.

Still, despite my brain's chatter, I kept practicing because it felt good to do it. Strange, new, but really good. I felt like I was literally pulling the cover off all of these little joys already there within my everyday life, but I'd completely ignored them until then. Of course, I was aware I liked coffee in the morning, time with my daughter was precious, and tulips were some of my favorite flowers (close tie for first place with peonies). But there's a huge difference between knowing you like certain things and actually *pausing to experience* the joy, comfort, and meaning they bring you.

NOTE TO SELF

When you are grateful
for the little things
they become the big things
that fuel you with
so much meaning.

I was finally allowing myself to experience that joy, comfort, and meaning fully, and not only did that feel really good but also it was softening some of my struggle. On really stressful days, I noticed that practicing Gratitude helped to buffer some of the stress—I still felt it, but it was less overwhelming. There was more light in my days; there were more moments of feeling okay. It was almost as if Gratitude was helping my brain to feel a little safer, not constantly on alert to notice all of the difficult, frustrating, and stressful stuff.

Gratitude turned out to be the *opposite* of what I had feared. It wasn't about glossing over problems or wearing rose-colored glasses and pretending everything was great when it wasn't. Practicing Gratitude was like putting on glasses for the first time after not being able to see very well. It brought to light so much goodness, joy, kindness, meaning, and sense of connection that were *already there in my life* but that I hadn't been able to experience. Gratitude wasn't about pretending—it was about uncovering.

Gratitude Is the Corrective Lens for Your Brain's Negativity Bias

Without practicing Gratitude, you have an incomplete emotional picture of your life, kind of like covering one eye with your hand.

Remember that because of your brain's negativity bias, you're much better at noticing and remembering anything negative than positive. So if you don't actively practice Gratitude, your brain is lying to you about your life—it distorts reality by exaggerating anything wrong, stressful, or annoying and minimizing stuff that's good or comforting.

When you practice Gratitude, you call your brain's bluff. You bring to light all the good stuff it was ignoring and fuel yourself with joy, comfort, and so much other awesomeness. Gratitude is literally a magic pill: the minute you focus your attention on something you appreciate, your brain releases serotonin, which not only gives you a mood boost but also increases your motivation and willpower. And research shows that after three weeks of practicing Gratitude consistently, new neural pathways are established in your brain, making it more natural for you to focus on what you appreciate.

So let's get to your focus practice, which I'm asking you to do every single morning this week. The way you begin your day has a huge impact on how the rest of your day goes, and starting with a Gratitude practice fuels your energy, helps you manage stress, and prevents your brain's negativity bias from taking over.

PRACTICE

Morning Gratitude Lens

Before reading your first email, social media post, or news article in the morning, think of three things you're grateful for.

Be genuine. Don't just tick off a bunch of things. Look at the moment or the day before through the Lens of Gratitude and find things you genuinely appreciate.

Be specific! This is one of the most important things about practicing Gratitude. If you keep your Gratitude general ("I'm grateful for my family" or "I'm grateful for my health"), your brain will just dismiss it. Ask yourself *why* you're grateful for your family or your health.

Smaller is better. Research shows that the frequency of small, positive life experiences rather than any huge accomplishments or experiences contributes to greater life satisfaction. So zoom in on the smallest things you appreciate!

Capture your Gratitude in some way. You don't need to keep a Gratitude journal if you're not the journaling type, but capturing your Gratitude helps your brain to take a better mental picture of it. You can jot down your Gratitude moments on an index card or in the Notes app on your phone, photograph what you're grateful for, and text or email your Gratitude to someone else.

Yes, variety is important. If you're always grateful for the same things, your brain will get used to them and stop caring. So don't get lazy; use your Gratitude Lens to look around at different parts of your life (e.g., things that happened yesterday, today, people you're grateful for, experiences, moments, foods, comforts, you name it!).

For extra Gratitude Hero credit, you can repeat this practice in the evening with your Evening Gratitude Lens. I know of no better way to interrupt my brain's chatter when I get into bed than by focusing on the things in my day for which I'm grateful.

There's a fun little story I heard, although I've not been able to find a record of it since. Perhaps it's one of those urban legends, but it's a great one, so I want to share it with you. It takes place in the mid-1930s, at the end of the Depression in the United States.

R. R. Donnelly was then a publishing and printing company (it's grown to do many other things since), and it had a hard time selling books. After the Depression, books weren't at the top of the list of household purchases. One of the marketing managers at the company had a friend whose company built houses. So he asked him to add built-in bookshelves to some of the homes they built.

What do you do when your home has built-in bookshelves? You buy books to fill them! As the story goes, this helped encourage more book sales.

When you practice your Morning Gratitude Lens, you build Gratitude bookshelves in your brain. You literally say to your brain, "Here are a few good things I appreciate, and now I want you to go look for more good things throughout the day."

Gratitude isn't difficult to practice. But if it's a new skill, your brain is not going to make it easy! The neural pathways it uses to notice the negative stuff are well established, and it's really good at using them.

Stay the course. Practice. And don't forget to talk back to your brain when it tries to sabotage your Gratitude practice.

Dear Brain: Please Stop Taking All the Good Stuff for Granted!

Have you ever gotten in your car to go home from work and suddenly you're home, but you can't remember anything about getting there? That's your brain's adaptability at work. In its efforts to protect you from danger, your brain doesn't want to waste its energy on stuff that's familiar because familiar is safe. Because you take the same or a similar way home every day, it's so familiar that your brain is on autopilot during your commute. It's almost as if the commute didn't happen.

Now, you might not care that your brain doesn't pay attention during your commute. But your brain's adaptability means that it also doesn't register many *good* familiar experiences. A hug from your kiddo when you walk through the door? If this happens often, your brain might not pause long enough to feel the warmth of this moment. That comforting cup of hot tea on a cold, rainy day? If you have tea every morning, your brain will completely ignore the joy and comfort of that experience unless you pause and appreciate it. When we say we take things for granted, this is what we mean: they become so familiar that our brain doesn't pay much attention to them, and they fade into the background.

When we moved to the house where we live now, the fridge was extremely loud. I'd sit in the kitchen having tea and get so annoyed at all the noises it was making. It drove me nuts!

After a few years, we got a new fridge. It was so quiet! For the first few weeks, every time I walked into the kitchen, I got excited about how quiet it was. But after a month or so, I got used to the quietness of the fridge. It became the new normal, familiar, something my brain now took for granted. I no longer got excited about how quiet it was when I walked into the kitchen, and worse, I started to complain about the dishwasher being too loud! Because the fridge was now quiet, I could hear the dishwasher better when it was on, so my brain's negativity bias went to work and began to remind me about this new annoying thing.

I'm sure you could come up with hundreds of examples just like this one from your own life, when something you were once excited or happy about became just another thing after you got used to it. What's worse, after you got used to it, you noticed many things about it you didn't like or that frustrated you. This happens with things like refrigerators, experiences like new jobs or trips, and people in our lives: the partner of your dreams turns out to be an actual human being with tons of imperfections that begin to annoy you after a few years together. (Right?)

This is why Gratitude is such an important skill to practice. It becomes the corrective lens that balances out your brain's adaptability and negativity bias and reminds you not to take for granted the good, positive, meaningful aspects of your life.

There's a concept in the Japanese language that I really love: *Ichigo-ichie*. It describes the idea of treasuring the moment because it's fleeting. Ichigo-ichie might be translated as "this moment we are in will never happen again." Actively practicing Gratitude helps us to treasure more moments in our lives, which makes our lives richer, fuller, and more meaningful. Instead of sprinting through our days and our to-do lists, we pause to experience the moments in our days and uncover sparkles of goodness, beauty, and joy within them. And this joy becomes part of the fuel that keeps us going through our marathon busy days and through the really hard ones.

How Gratitude Can Help You When Life Sucks

We've all had those days that begin with a small annoyance that snowballs into making it a terrible, no-good, very bad day. You spill your coffee, yell at your kids, get stuck in traffic, get annoyed at your colleague because she seems happy while you're annoyed, send the email to the wrong person, get an annoyed email from your boss who heard from that person . . . and before you know it, your brain has convinced you that the world is out to get you, and this is a horrible day.

Ugh, I hate those days. They feel like an endless, frustrating spiral you can't control.

It turns out that when you're stressed out, your brain's negativity bias goes into overdrive, becoming even more sensitive to anything that's wrong, annoying, or stressful. Negativity actually begets negativity, which is why it's hard to turn around a crappy day. But you can do it with Gratitude.

Here's my favorite practice to help you pause a negative thought spiral or feel less overwhelmed with stress or frustration.

PRACTICE

Gratitude Antidote

When you feel overwhelmed or your brain is taking you down a negativity spiral, pause, take a deep breath, acknowledge how you feel, and then think of three specific things you're grateful for.

Remember to be specific with your Gratitude.

Three is a made-up number, but the idea is that you want to think of a bunch of things. Your brain's negativity bias is really strong when you're stressed out, and you need to power up your Gratitude to counter it.

I'm not asking you to be grateful for whatever is stressing you out. That would be cruel. The goal is to redirect your brain's attention from overwhelm to Gratitude, so thinking of anything you genuinely feel grateful for is great.

Here are a few examples of how this might work in practice:

Stressful Thought	Gratitude Antidote
I'm so overwhelmed with all the stuff I need to get done today.	"I'm so overwhelmed with all the stuff I need to get done today . . . BUT I'm grateful that I had a good breakfast this morning, so I have some energy and fuel. The sun is shining, so I can take a little walk outside as a short break, and I get to drink tea from my favorite mug."
I feel guilty that I missed my son's bedtime because I had to work late.	"I feel guilty that I missed my son's bedtime because I had to work late . . . BUT I'm grateful that I gave him a hug this morning. The weekend is in a few days, and we get to hang out together. And I finally got the tough project done at work."
Everything is going wrong today.	"This day is definitely not going my way . . . BUT I'm grateful to be inside while it's pouring out. It was so nice to hear from my friend earlier today. And in a few hours, I get to collapse into bed and this no good, very bad day will be over."

Making it through a tough day is one thing, but when you're facing a difficult challenge or you're really struggling, your brain's overactive negativity bias can undermine your ability to make it through. In these toughest moments, your practice of Gratitude becomes your lifeline.

A few years ago, Laura, one of my dearest lifelong friends, was going through a really rough time. She had been dealing with health issues on and off for years, and after a procedure that offered to relieve what was left of them failed to deliver, her hope and resolve plunged. She was in pain and exhausted.

I was desperate to find a way to help, even though we lived on opposite sides of the country. So I suggested that every day we would text each other a few things we were grateful for. I knew Gratitude was new for Laura, and she was, as I had been, a Gratitude skeptic. But I nudged her to give it a try.

For the next several months, we kept up our Gratitude texts almost daily. Some days I would text her and wouldn't

NOTE TO SELF

Sometimes life sucks.
But when you practice
gratitude
amidst the suck
it gives you strength
to keep going.

get a reply, but other days she would be the first to text me her Gratitude moments. When we saw each other a year later, Laura told me that our daily Gratitude texts were a lifeline that kept her going during that incredibly difficult time.

When your brain perceives danger, which it does whenever you're facing a challenge, its focus narrows: it just wants to think about this challenge because that way, it figures it can protect you from danger. And to give itself a sense of certainty within uncertainty, this is when your brain also wastes your energy with ruminating on all the worst-case scenarios. I remember that at one point, Laura asked me if she would ever feel better—she had struggled for so long, she wasn't sure it was possible.

But when, within the challenge, you look for things you appreciate, you remind your brain that there is more to your life than just the difficulties you're facing. You literally widen the lens through which your brain perceives your reality to include what is good or just okay alongside what is difficult and stressful. Doing this helps the brain to feel a little safer and calmer, not so overwhelmed with negative thoughts and difficult feelings. And this, in turn, helps to boost your emotional and mental energy so you can use that energy to get through whatever challenge you're facing.

After I did a workshop on the power of Gratitude for doctors and nurses at Massachusetts General Hospital, Hemal, one of the doctors, shared something that stayed with me. He told me that before they began their patient rounds, one of the other doctors in the group always shared something he is grateful for. Sometimes it was really small, like having hot water in the shower. But hearing this doctor's expression of Gratitude always inspired Hemal to think of things he appreciated, and that, in turn, gave him fuel and strength to face the pain and suffering of the patients he cared for.

You can't be grateful for everything in your life. Some moments and experiences are painful, difficult, stressful, and even traumatic. Sometimes life just sucks. But when you practice Gratitude and look for something good, however small, within the suck, it gives you the fuel and strength to keep going.

Gratitude's Unexpected Power: Muting Your Inner Critic

The same way your brain lies to you about your reality because it overfocuses on what's wrong and takes for granted the good stuff that's familiar, it lies to you about YOU. Yep, you heard me right. That inner critic in overdrive in your brain? It's ignoring good stuff about you because it takes it for granted and it focuses way too much attention on everything supposedly wrong with you—and blows it all out of proportion.

This is a really important thing to recognize, so I want you to pause and think about it for a minute. (I'll wait.) Just as your brain doesn't give you an objective picture of your life because of its negativity bias, familiar thinking patterns, and adaptability, it doesn't give you an objective picture of *you*. And your inner critic grabs on to that incorrect information and makes you feel like crap.

How do you change that? By turning the Lens of Gratitude onto yourself.

When was the last time you actively appreciated something about yourself? If you're like most Awesome Humans I know, the answer is going to be disappointing. We don't do this often or nearly often enough. So no wonder our inner critic is a lot louder than our self-appreciator: we spend a lot more mental energy focusing on our flaws, imperfections, and apparent inadequacies than our strengths, unique quirks, and awesomeness. I can confidently say that my inner critic, combined with my inner doubter, steals more of my energy than anything else. And our culture definitely doesn't help: somehow it's cool to be self-deprecating, but saying good things about yourself is considered bragging.

I want to change that! So here's a practice I would love for you to embrace wholeheartedly this week. I initially made it up for myself when I got really sick of being told—by my own brain!—about all the ways I wasn't good enough, amazing, or perfect. (It's a great practice to combine with Calling BS on Your Brain's "Not Good Enough" Stories!)

PRACTICE

Gratitude Swap

Whenever your inner critic pipes up with yet another self-criticism, think of something you're grateful for about yourself.

Your self-gratitude can be for a quality you have or something you've done (or not done, like not snapping at your kids, who are driving you nuts). As with your other Gratitude practices, remember to be specific. And when your brain pipes up with a counterargument to your self-gratitude, please feel free to tell it to shut up. And yes, you gotta put your bossy pants on when you do this!

AWESOME HUMAN AWARD

I know how challenging it is to quiet your inner critic, so after you successfully practice the Gratitude Swap, please excitedly give yourself the **Putting My Inner Critic on Mute** award. This is serious progress!

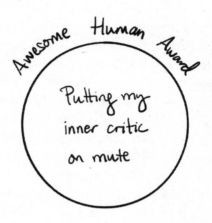

The Magic of Generously Sharing Gratitude with Others

One of the most powerful and beautiful ways to practice Gratitude is to express your appreciation to other people. Just as pausing to be grateful for ordinary moments fuels you with a bit of joy and comfort, sharing your Gratitude with others turns ordinary interactions into more meaningful connections. It makes life less transactional and helps you to feel less alone, which is essential to bringing out your inner Awesome Human.

Last year, my family and I stayed in a hotel in San Francisco. We have this fun little tradition we call Family Awards, where we give each other random, silly awards, like Best Putter Together of IKEA Furniture (currently held by my daughter). Before we left the hotel one morning, my daughter and my husband wrote me a Best Mama Even Though She Is Tired award on hotel stationery. (I'd done three speaking engagements in two days and was definitely tired.)

When we came back later that day, there was a tray of chocolate-covered strawberries waiting for us, with a note from housekeeping that they wanted to sweeten my day even more. They must have seen the award note my husband and daughter had left.

I was so grateful for this act of kindness! I got the name of the hotel manager and sent her an email of gratitude that I asked her to share with the housekeeping staff who had left the treat for us. The next morning, she wrote back to say that she read my note out loud during the staff meeting, and it meant so much to the two women who surprised us.

After exchanging a few emails, my husband, daughter, and I went down to meet the hotel manager and general manager, just to say hello and thank them in person for creating a culture of kindness within their team. We chatted for a while, and they even took us to their executive offices to show us their Gratitude Boards, where they kept all the notes of Gratitude staff members wrote to each other. Gratitude was something the entire staff at the hotel practiced and valued. Research shows that teams who practice Gratitude at work create better experiences for customers, and here we were, literally living through one of those awesome experiences.

When we got in the car to drive to the airport and fly back home to Boston, I felt like we were leaving a familiar and warm place and friends, not a hotel with staff we didn't know. This is the magical power of sharing your gratitude with others: it weaves a fabric of human connection and helps to make the most ordinary experiences a little more meaningful and warmer.

As you practice your Gratitude skills this week, I invite you to become more intentional and more generous in expressing Gratitude to others. Here's a practice to guide you.

PRACTICE

Look at Others Through the Gratitude Lens

As you go through your week, focus on finding opportunities to express gratitude to people with whom you interact. Intentionally look at them through the Lens of Gratitude to notice something they might have done that supported or uplifted you in some way and then share your appreciation with them.

A few tips:

You can tell the person you appreciate them in person, send a text or an email, or even write an actual note. Share your Gratitude in whatever way feels most authentic to you.

Be specific. Tell the person *why* you appreciate them.

You don't need to use the word *Gratitude* if it doesn't feel right! Find your own words. What matters is that your Gratitude is genuine; no one cares about the specific words you use.

Here's an email I sent to my colleague Debbie on a recent Friday, to give you an example:

"I know it was a nutty week, and I really appreciate you staying on top of all the things and details so I could focus on the big talks and my book edits. THANK YOU!!! #goteam"

A great way to make sharing Gratitude with others a regular practice (versus something you do only when you remember) is to create a little ritual around it. Here are a few ideas to get you started, but please feel free to make up your own and kick it off this week!

Simple Gratitude Sharing Rituals

Monday Gratitude	Start the week by thinking about a few people you appreciate, and write them short little notes of gratitude (could be your family, friends, colleagues, etc.). I like to write notes on small, colorful pieces of paper and leave them for my daughter and husband to find on Monday mornings.
Gratitude Buddies	Ask a friend, colleague, or family member to be your Gratitude Buddy, and agree on how you'll share daily or weekly Gratitude with each other (texts or emails work great!).
Gratitude Tag	This is awesome for families, especially with young kids: over dinner, share something you're grateful for, or your gratitude for someone else at the table, and then tag another person to go next.

The Gratitude Glue for Relationships

Expressing Gratitude to others not only makes ordinary interactions more joyful and meaningful but also strengthens relationships. Research shows that when people regularly express gratitude toward each other, they create a foundation of trust, and their relationships are more resilient through challenging times.

I can 1,000 percent attest to this being true for me and my husband. We went through a really difficult period in our marriage that, not surprisingly, coincided with my burnout. (One thing I learned is that when you feel darkness inside, it seeps into every area of your life, including your relationships.)

Becoming intentional about sharing our gratitude toward each other has become a core part of the fabric of connection we've re-created.

Often our gratitude is for really tiny things. The other day I wrote my husband a note that said, "Thank you for opening all the packages!" I hate opening packages! I can never easily open them, and it's a battle every time. My family lovingly makes fun of me for this, and yes, there are even videos because, according to them, no one opens packages quite like I do. The battle is real! So my husband opens all the packages delivered to our house to save me the battle . . . I mean the trouble.

Sometimes, our gratitude is for bigger life stuff. It's not *what* we're grateful for that's made a difference but regularly looking at each other through the Lens of Gratitude and then actively sharing our appreciation for each other. Yes, of course there are still a bajillion things Avi does that drive me up the wall, and the same is true of me for him! (If you must know, I sometimes take bites of things and leave the rest in the fridge, and Avi doesn't seem to have the gene that allows him to clean up his desk all the way. These are just two of our little loving annoyances.) And we are human beings, so of course we get upset with each other and frustrated and all the other human emotions, especially after twenty-four years of being together. But I can unequivocally say that developing our mutual Gratitude practice and looking for things to be grateful for in each other has helped the good stuff take more space in our heads and hearts than the annoying or frustrating habits.

Regularly expressing gratitude has another important benefit: it helps us have more honest and sometimes tough conversations.

Lauren is a leader and Awesome Human I've been lucky to work with, and she told me that because her team members share gratitude with each other regularly, they are more open to hearing challenging feedback. They know their colleagues value them and their contributions, so instead of questioning their worth or wondering if this difficult feedback means they suck at their jobs, their brains feel safe enough to receive it for what it is: feedback that will help them improve.

That's really powerful!

Every time you express gratitude for someone else, you tell them "I see you, I value you, and I recognize your contribution." Being on the receiving end of Gratitude makes us feel what psychologists call "socially valued." And when we feel socially valued, we are more motivated and resilient.

It's Okay If You Feel Awkward Practicing Gratitude at Work (Do It Anyway)

I can't finish this chapter without a quick encouragement to bring your practice of Gratitude to work with you this week. And I totally get it if it feels awkward. That's okay!

It's completely normal, actually, especially if it's not something you've done before or seen others do at work.

My advice is to fully own the fact that it feels weird or uncomfortable. Acknowledge it. I guarantee you that you're not the only person at work who feels weird about expressing Gratitude to your colleagues. So when you acknowledge that it feels weird, you might encourage others to share more gratitude even when they feel weird about it.

You might say something like:

> "I know I haven't done this kind of thing before, but I want to tell you that I really appreciate . . ."

> "I am trying to be more intentional about expressing gratitude, which is new for me, and I feel a bit awkward about it, so I want to tell you that . . ."

> "Okay, to be honest, I feel out of my element doing this, but here goes: . . ."

And you are always free to use me: *"I read this awesome book, and the awesome author said we should practice more gratitude at work, so I'm doing it even though it feels a little weird."* (Okay, you don't need to say awesome so much—one time is great.)

Remember that Gratitude is a skill, and when you're learning a new skill, it's supposed to feel awkward, weird, and uncomfortable! The only way for it to feel less so is by practicing it a lot. So tap into your courage, remind yourself about all the benefits, and embrace your inner Gratitude Hero this week!

Practices in This Chapter

Morning Gratitude Lens
Gratitude Antidote
Gratitude Swap
Look at Others Through the Gratitude Lens

Your Note to Self
What is something you want to remember, practice, or reflect on from this chapter?

AWESOME HUMAN AWARD

After you complete this week by doing at least one gratitude practice daily, give yourself the **Gratitude Hero** award! I hope it inspires you to create a lifelong gratitude habit!

CHAPTER 11

Week 3—Self-Care

This week you're going to become a No-Guilt Self-Care Warrior, so let's start by getting our terms straight.

What do you think of when you hear the word *self-care*? I'll tell you what I used to think: self-care was that thing other people did because they weren't strong enough to just power through, like me, or because they'd done enough to earn it, which I absolutely had not. Mostly, I thought of self-care as going to a spa and getting massages, and those just felt like indulgences I couldn't allow myself to enjoy because how could I spend time and money on myself when I had work and family to take care of? I felt way too guilty to do that.

Unfortunately, my old view of self-care isn't unique—so many people I've worked with are trapped by it. So let's start by getting rid of any ideas you might have around self-care being a luxury, an indulgence, or a reward you need to earn or deserve somehow by doing enough, working enough, or struggling enough.

It has nothing to do with any of that.

Self-care is the skill of fueling your emotional, mental, and physical energy.

Your energy is your fuel.

Would you expect a car to be able to run without fuel? No. The car doesn't either "deserve" fuel or not. It *needs* fuel to function. It can't do its job of being a car without fuel.

Same is true for us Awesome Humans: We can't function without energy. We can't do all the things we need and want to do and *do them well and for a long time* without having enough emotional, mental, and physical energy. We can't do our job of being human without fuel.

And Self-Care is the skill of making sure we have enough of it. Does that sound like an indulgence?

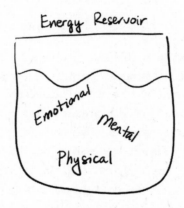

You start each day with a limited reservoir of emotional, mental, and physical energy. All the things you do throughout the day require your energy, so they deplete your reservoir. Some of these things are external, like work tasks, conversations with people, and home responsibilities; some of them are internal, like your thoughts and self-talk.

When you practice Self-Care, you intentionally do things to fill your energy reservoir and limit doing things that *unnecessarily* drain it. This second part is so important, but it doesn't get nearly enough oomph when we talk about Self-Care. So let's start with it!

You Can't Fill a Leaky Reservoir

Think of it this way: your best efforts to fuel your energy won't get you very far if there are too many leaks in your reservoir.

Of course, you can't stop working or taking care of your responsibilities. I'm not suggesting that at all. But there are plenty of things that drain your energy that you *could* do less or a little bit less. Here are a few energy drains I'm willing to bet you could reduce:

- Multitasking

- Mindlessly scrolling social media

- Overconsuming news

- Talking negatively to and about yourself

- Trying to do things perfectly

- Making tons of decisions (and trying to make each one perfectly)

Making tons of decisions throughout the day was perpetually one of my big energy drainers. I wasted so much energy being a control freak and thought that every decision needed two things:

1. Me

2. My agonizing over it

I suffered from decision fatigue, although, boy, did I resist acknowledging this! Decision fatigue is a big energy drain for many people because every single decision you make requires your energy, from what you're going to wear today, to what task to work on next, to what to make for dinner, to what show to watch, and on and on and on.

Steve Jobs wore a daily uniform of jeans and a black turtleneck because he didn't want to waste energy choosing a different outfit every day. Picking out what to wear isn't a decision I want to give up—it's fun for me!—but burning out did force me to get more intentional and disciplined about prioritizing decisions and recognizing when a decision is not important enough for me to care about it.

Learning How to Manage Your Energy Reservoir

Your main challenge this week is to become more aware of your emotional, mental, and physical energy levels and commit to a consistent, daily Self-Care practice that fuels your reservoir and reduces unnecessary drains.

I recently wrote about the energy reservoir in my weekly Happier email, and a woman wrote back saying it made her realize that she only practiced Self-Care after she crashed and burned from endless overworking.

Wow, that hit home. For most of my life, my "practice" of Self-Care involved getting so exhausted that I couldn't run through my day at the same frantic pace and I had to get a few more hours of sleep or zone out on the couch in the evening for a few hours of watching TV. I never paused to check on my energy levels during the day, so it was only when I felt completely burned out that I slowed down. Eventually, as I've shared with you, my daily burnout snowballed into one huge, life-pausing, scary burnout. I couldn't function anymore—I had not a single drop of energy left.

When the car runs out of gas, it stops. When you run out of energy, you stop.

I meet so many people who live right on the edge of burnout, running on nearly empty energy reserves. I lived that way for so long that I can sense it in other people without them saying anything. You know that you can't keep going like this, but you don't know how and what to change. It feels like a trap.

But running on almost empty doesn't just feel terrible—it also prevents you from being good at the things you care about. You can't be great at your job if you're exhausted and depleted, just as you can't be a great parent or friend.

My car fuel tank comparison turns out to be a good one: in most cars, when the fuel tank is less than one-quarter full, the fuel pump has to strain more, and the car becomes less fuel efficient. (This is almost the entirety of my car knowledge, so please don't expect much more.) If you're always running on an almost-empty energy reservoir, you have to strain more doing any task, which takes even more of your energy, creating a destructive cycle.

Think about the simplest example, like writing an email to your colleague. When you're exhausted, it's harder to focus, it takes you more time, and you can't express yourself as well as when you feel fueled. A ton of research shows how depleted emotional, mental, or physical energy negatively affects our ability to think clearly, make good decisions, and solve problems.

This brings me to another reason to make Self-Care a regular daily practice rather than holding off until you "really need it." And I gotta tell you, the efficiency lover in me is really excited to share this with you:

When you practice Self-Care *consistently* and keep your energy reservoir fueled most of the time, your Self-Care practice takes less time. Think about filling up your car: when your tank is empty, it takes longer to fill it up than when there's some gas already in it. When your energy reservoir is empty, it takes more time and effort to fill it up. It took me several years to heal from my burnout, and I had to put much of my life on pause while I did it. Several. Years.

But if you top off your energy reservoir daily, it takes less time and effort each time, which means it's easier to fit into your busy schedule. It's an awesome, constructive cycle: when you practice regularly, you need less time for your practice, so you're more likely to do it even when you have a ton going on!

Sure, sometimes you can't help it, and you've got to go all out. You've got a huge project at work, a loved one needs your care, the basement floods . . . or all three at the same time. (I am speaking from experience here.) When that happens, your energy reservoir can get close to empty. But if you've been practicing Self-Care consistently, you'll know how to refuel quickly.

So, let's get practicing. Your first step in mastering the skill of Self-Care is to become aware of your emotional, mental, and physical energy reservoir on a daily basis. Think of it as making sure your car has fuel.

Here's your focus practice for this week.

PRACTICE

Lens of Self-Care

Your focus for this week is to look at yourself through the Lens of Self-Care by becoming aware of your emotional, mental, and physical energy reservoir levels daily and then doing more of what fuels your energy and less of what drains it unnecessarily.

Start with doing this practice once a day—in the morning, midday, or evening. Put a reminder on your calendar so you don't forget to do it. As you get the hang of it, begin to practice it throughout the day.

Here are three questions to ask yourself:

1: How is my emotional, mental, and physical energy reservoir right now?

Be specific: you might be emotionally drained but physically fueled or the other way around.

As with emotional awareness, whatever comes up is the right answer. Don't judge yourself (less "I shouldn't feel so tired!" and more "I feel physically tired!").

2: What has been unnecessarily draining my energy today, and can I do it less?

Again, get specific. "Work" is not a good answer—it's too general, and you can't learn anything from it that will help you. Is there something specific about work that has been draining that you *could* reduce? For example, are you stuck on a task and asking someone for help might do the trick?

If you notice that you're emotionally or mentally drained, take a moment to practice Struggle Awareness and the Lens of Acceptance to help shift your thoughts so they drain less energy.

3: What can I do to fill my energy reservoir today?

Small things count: a five-minute walk outside can do a lot for your energy (we'll talk about this more in a bit).

More specific = better. "Relax" is meh. "Sit down and read for a half hour with my favorite cup of tea after dinner" is better.

Self-Care Means Learning How to Say No

I think most of us think about Self-Care as doing something—taking a walk, relaxing with a book, doing some yoga, journaling, and many other wonderful things. But I want to talk about one of the toughest Self-Care practices: *saying no to doing something that drains your energy.*

Saying no to a friend who invites you to go out when you're tired.

Saying no to your brain when it tells you that you must do something perfectly or like you have always done it.

Saying no to a colleague who asks for your help when your own to-do list is overwhelming.

Let's acknowledge the elephant in the room: saying no is really hard. We don't want to disappoint people, we are afraid we'll miss out on something, and we're afraid of hurting other people's feelings.

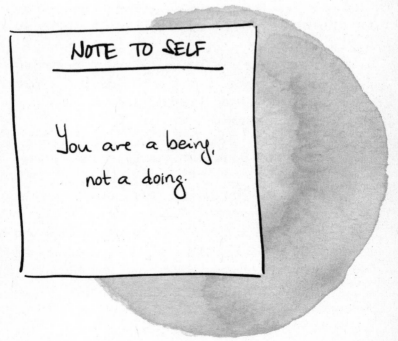

NOTE TO SELF

You are a being,
not a doing.

I'm a people pleaser in recovery, and it took my fully burning out to get honest about it. I used to feel that I needed to earn the love and respect of other people by constantly doing things for them and never, ever, ever saying no.

My teacher once told me that I was a being, not a doing. She said I didn't have to over-effort all the time to earn the love of people I cared about, that my being was enough.

This felt true, but it was hard to accept because I'd spent my life over-efforting at everything. It was strange to think of my *being* as enough (and believe me, my brain did a fantastic job reminding me of all the ways I wasn't enough!). And yet when I think about my friends, family, and other people I care about, I recognize that they bring a lot of goodness, meaning, and comfort to me without doing anything—*just by being.*

Of course, I appreciate it when my husband makes me tea in the morning or my daughter goes to the store with me because she knows I like her company. Their acts of kindness are meaningful, and it's important that they take on their share of responsibilities at home, so we all pitch in. (Plus, according to my husband, I am completely incompetent at loading the dishwasher correctly, so obviously I can't be in charge of doing it!)

But my husband and my daughter—just like other people I love—don't *need* to do anything for me to love them or to feel comfort and joy from their being in my life. Their being in my life is enough. If I ask my daughter to go to the store with me and she says no, I don't love her any less. I might get a little bummed out, but it doesn't in any way impact how I feel about her or how invaluable she is to my life.

In a world that celebrates doing and accomplishing so much, it's easy to forget that our mere being and presence have intrinsic value, but this is exactly what I am asking you to remember. When you do, it will make it a little easier to learn how to say no when you can't energetically afford doing something other Awesome Humans are asking you to do—or you feel they're expecting you to do.

This idea of being able to energetically afford something is really helpful to me, so I want to highlight it. When there's something you want to buy, you think about whether you can afford it. **When there's something you're thinking of doing or someone is asking you to do, part of your consideration has to be whether you can energetically afford it.** Core to practicing Self-Care skills is being aware of your emotional, mental, and physical energy and making your energy part of your decision-making process for what, when, and how you do something.

I recently interviewed Morra Aarons-Mele for my Awesome Human Hour weekly show, and we got to talk about setting boundaries to avoid burning out. Morra has an intense job; hosts a podcast; is a best-selling author; and oh, is also a mom of three. So, she has a few things on her plate. I mentioned to her that one of my boundaries is creating "no-calls" days.

Mondays and Fridays are my no-calls days, and although, of course, I end up making exceptions from time to time, I try to keep them free from calls or presentations. I need swaths of empty time to get into deep thinking and creativity, so I guard these days as much as I can.

As I was sharing this with Morra, she asked me whether I actually respected myself enough to stick to my no-calls commitment on Mondays and Fridays. She shared that she tries to block off uninterrupted time but finds it challenging to stick to.

"I start to worry about disappointing people, like my clients. And as someone who runs her own business, there's the worry that if I block off a day and say no to an opportunity, maybe more opportunities won't come my way," she said.

I totally get that. Sometimes I worry that by blocking off days, I'll miss out on a great speaking gig or annoy my colleague Debbie, who is more of a phone person than I am (although after a few years of working together, I've learned to find joy in our conversations, a big achievement for this lifelong phone-call hater! All credit for this goes to Debbie). But my awareness that I simply can't afford to spend energy talking on the phone if I want to have energy to think and write helps me stick to my no-calls commitments most of the time. I respect myself by respecting the reality that I don't have unlimited energy, and I need to make trade-offs about where I spend it.

NOTE TO SELF

Practicing self-care means sometimes saying no so you have energy to do what's most meaningful to you.

You don't have unlimited energy. So when you need to summon up your courage to say no to someone or something because you can't energetically afford to say yes, think about how preserving your energy will help you do more of what's meaningful and important to you.

If you say yes to going out with a friend when you feel tired, will you have enough fuel to get your work done the next day without burning out?

If you say yes to cleaning your house until it's "perfect" according to your standards, will you have enough energy to be present with your family?

I like to think of setting boundaries less as saying no to something and more as saying yes to what is most important to me. What helps me set and actually respect them is to remind myself *why* protecting my energy is important to me. I usually cook dinner during the week, but when I'm feeling drained, I tell my family that we're having a floor picnic instead. This means eating takeout or random stuff from the fridge sitting on the floor of our living room while watching a show. The old me would see this as failure to be a good mom and wife, but now I know that if I skip cooking, I will have more energy to actually be a pleasant human being for my husband and daughter.

You're not a machine. You can't do all things perfectly, always. Practicing Self-Care means making trade-offs and choices and being courageously honest with yourself—and with others!— about doing less when you don't have enough energy to spare.

Here's a quick practice to help you do this. Think of it as your shorthand for figuring out if you can energetically afford to do something.

PRACTICE

No/Yes Trade-Off

When you recognize that you need to say no to something to preserve your energy but your brain is piling on guilt or fear, use this little practice to help you get clarity around your WHY for setting this boundary.

I need to say NO to _____

so that I can say YES to _____

_____

Be really honest with yourself about what you're saying yes to. More energy? Avoiding burning out or feeling overwhelmed? More time with your family or more time to get work done? More joy? Just because your soul is crying out for some quiet time? There are no wrong answers.

AWESOME HUMAN AWARD

Saying no to protect your energy is one of the toughest practices to master. So after you've done this practice successfully a few times, I want you to proudly give yourself the **Mastering the Art of Saying No** award!

Reducing Mindless Energy Drainers (Yep, We Need to Talk about Your Social Media Scrolling)

I would be a terrible guide for your Awesome Human Project if I didn't offer you advice for how to reduce energy drain from two of the most common culprits: mindlessly scrolling social media and overconsuming the news.

First, I've got zero judgment. We all do too much of both. I could write many paragraphs to explain why, but the "too long; didn't read" (TLDR) version is that in search of quick rewards, our brains have created some unhelpful habit loops:

Trigger: "I am bored!" "I am stressed!"

Action: Check social media or the news

Reward: A quick hit of dopamine

Here's the problem: that hit of dopamine is really small and wears off fast, but the cost of being stuck in these habit loops is high. You already know that mindlessly scrolling social media drains your energy and makes you feel like crap. (Research also shows it can increase anxiety and risk of depression, especially if you're endlessly scrolling without engaging by, say, leaving a comment on someone's post.)

So, what can you do?

I'll get right to the answer: question the reward.

Researchers including Judson Brewer, whose work on reducing anxiety I'm a big fan of, have found that becoming more mindful and asking yourself how the action you're doing is making you feel helps you break unhealthy habit loops. It's kind of like saying to your brain: "Listen, you think checking social media one hundred times a day will make me feel good, but does it really? No!"

The more you do this, the more your brain will stop seeing that action as one that brings you rewards, and boom, you will break the habit loop!

Here's THE question I want you to ask yourself a LOT this week when you get caught doing something that drains your energy—like social media and news scrolling:

"Does this fuel me, or does this drain me?"

The answer will come quickly. Your job is to be open to it, acknowledge it, and make sure your brain heard it. You CAN break the habit loops that drain your energy, as long as you practice.

How to Limit Energy Drain from Difficult People

Whenever I speak about Self-Care and doing less of what drains your energy, the most frequent question I get is this: What can I do if I live or work with someone who drains my energy by being abrasive, negative, rude, or even toxic?

This is really tough. You know by now that human emotions are contagious, so you can't eliminate the effect this difficult person has on you. Although I don't have a magic formula that can eliminate this drain from your life, I do have a few specific suggestions:

- When you interact with these people, remind yourself that you do not have to take on their feelings. You can listen and be empathetic, but you don't need to take them on.

- Think about what these people might be struggling with that's causing them to act this way. This is an advanced practice, and I'll share much more about it in chapter 12, on Intentional Kindness. When you imagine how others might be struggling and choose not to react as opposed to lashing out with anger or annoyance, you get to protect your energy. And that's your number one goal.

- After a difficult or negative interaction, do something to intentionally fuel your energy. Write down a few things you're grateful for, take a quick walk outside, check in on a friend.

- If you find yourself ruminating on a difficult conversation you've had, ask yourself: *Is this helpful to me?* The answer is never a yes, so when you get explicit about it, you can choose to shift your thoughts in a different direction.

- If you're dealing with someone toxic, limit your interactions with this person as much as possible. Even if you can talk to this person a little less, it's a win.

And here's the really hard thing I want to tell you: if it is possible to stop interacting with someone who constantly drains your energy, consider doing it. It's not going to be easy, and your brain will try to make you feel guilty and tell you all kinds of stories about how this is your fault for not being patient enough or understanding enough. But if you truly feel that this person drains your energy, you will find a way to talk back to your brain.

When I was starting my journey out of burnout, my teacher told me that some people in my life weren't going to come with me. At the time, I was just fighting to get through the day, so I didn't pay much attention to her words. But she was right: a few people didn't come on my journey with me.

In most cases, this was a mutual choice. I realized that interacting with them was only draining my energy, and for all kinds of reasons I can only imagine, they realized that our friendship wasn't valuable anymore. This is just a guess, but for a few friends, my not always being in crisis and struggle mode simply became boring.

Not everyone will come with you on your journey of learning to struggle less and embrace your Awesome Human. And it will be difficult to lose some relationships with friends or family members and recognize that they weren't rooted in genuine care and mutual respect and support. But your choice is between staying in struggle and draining your energy or choosing to live with less struggle so you have more energy to bring to everything that's meaningful to you. Tap into your courage to get honest with yourself about what truly matters, and the choice will be a little easier to make.

The Case for No-Guilt Self-Care

Now that we've talked about doing less of the stuff that drains you, it's time to dive into the other part of your energy-fueling equation: practicing Self-Care to fill your emotional, mental, and physical energy reservoir.

And we can't talk about this without addressing the biggest obstacle that prevents most Awesome Humans I know from doing this: guilt.

I hear this so often:

> "I have too many things I need to do, so I feel guilty about doing things I want to do for me."

> "I can't take time for self-care because other people need me."

First, I get you. I'm really good at guilt, especially around doing something for myself when my brain is yelling at me that I should be doing work or caring for other people.

When my daughter was little, I couldn't possibly imagine doing something as absurd as taking time away from her to do something just for me. Go to a yoga class on the weekend when I could be with her? What a crazy idea! After she turned two, I did fit in a spin class here and there on the weekend, but I felt guilty for the entirety of the fifty-five minutes I was spinning and sweating and not hanging out with my daughter. (Does guilt help you burn more calories?)

Because I thought it was the greatest sin as a mom to serve my daughter anything but home-cooked meals, even while I was working full-time in really intense jobs, I would do a cooking marathon every Sunday evening. After she went to bed and I caught up on some work, I would make three or four meals for the week ahead.

I remember how deeply exhausted I felt while chopping, mixing, and cooking in the kitchen late at night. I also remember how proud of myself I was for making this sacrifice for my daughter. I *could* be resting or sleeping, but here I was being a supermom and cooking her these amazing gourmet meals! In some way, I derived satisfaction from sacrificing my well-being for my daughter. The martyr mom identity fit me nicely, and it was like an antidote to guilt: I still felt guilty when I was away from my daughter, but because I sacrificed my well-being to take good care of her, the guilt felt less severe.

I exhausted myself with my over-efforting on cooking, and that exhaustion came out in the form of snapping at my family, being annoyed at every little thing, and bringing this heavy cloud into our lives.

It hurts to acknowledge this, but I share this painful lesson because getting honest with myself helped me embrace no-guilt Self-Care. (Okay, *most of the time* no-guilt Self-Care.)

When you neglect your Self-Care, you bring depleted, low, stress-fueled energy to every single person with whom you interact, whether you want to or not. Is that what you want to do? Of course, the answer is no. So tell that to your guilt!

In fact, I want to go further: **practicing Self-Care is an act of love toward people you care about.** If there's any part of you that doubts this, ask them.

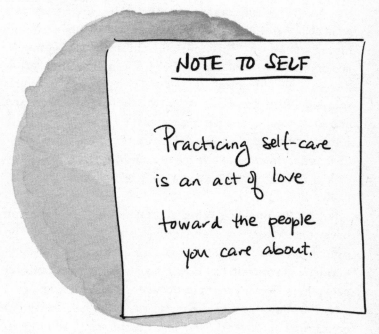

NOTE TO SELF

Practicing self-care is an act of love toward the people you care about.

Seriously, go ask your coworkers or your family members how they feel when you take care of yourself and how they feel when you don't. I did this before I set out to write this book: I asked my daughter what it felt like when I never took time for myself.

She responded, "It was kinda tense in the house, to be honest. You would, like, snap for no reason or some really small reason and then feel bad, and I felt bad, and then you would apologize and feel so sad! Small things really seemed to set you off, like when I was cutting a tomato with a non-serrated knife."

Yes, you read this right: I would snap at my daughter for using the wrong knife to cut tomatoes because I denied myself all Self-Care. I was so overwhelmed, and my emotional buffer was so thin that a tiny thing like that would cause me to over-react and snap at her.

Was this painful to hear? Yes. Was it an amazing reminder that practicing Self-Care is not optional? Big yes! I asked Mia what changed after I began to practice Self-Care and do things I loved just for me. "The atmosphere in the house became relaxed, you know?" she said, in the most genuine, unrehearsed, teenage way. "When something goes wrong, you focus on the solution versus freaking out. You are more chill and relaxed, and so we are, too, and it's just better."

It's just better. We fall into this trap of thinking that Self-Care and taking care of others are a zero-sum game: when we do something to fuel ourselves, we're taking something away from others.

But it's the opposite. When you take care of yourself, you have a bigger reservoir of energy to give to people you love and care about. **You can't take good care of others if you don't take care of yourself.** Just like a leader, you can't positively impact others' capacity to thrive if you don't fuel yours first.

Maybe you can do it for a short time, until your energy reservoir runs out. But you can't do it *sustainably*. And my bet is that the people you care about want your care for a long time, in a *sustainable* way. I'm certain that my husband and my daughter would have been happy to eat frozen meals for dinner if that meant having a wife and mom who wasn't on the edge of burnout daily.

You can't give what you don't have.

I share this reminder with you again because I don't think we can say this to ourselves enough. It's the best counterargument when our brains overwhelm us with guilt around Self-Care.

But I want you to make it even stronger by getting specific about ways in which your practice of Self-Care benefits the people you care about.

PRACTICE

Write a No-Guilt, Self-Care, Talk Back to Your Brain Script

If I could live in your brain and give it a pep talk every time it tried to make you feel guilty about practicing Self-Care, I would. But I can't—mostly good news for you—so I want you to write your own Talk Back to Your Brain Script and use it to give yourself a pep talk.

Step 1: Make a list of ways your Self-Care benefits other people.

Be specific: For example, "I'm more patient with my kids after I do some yoga," or "I'm more patient with my colleagues when I'm energized."

I encourage you—dare you!—to ask a few Awesome Humans in your life about how they feel when you've taken care of yourself and when you haven't (as I did with my daughter).

Step 2: Write a short Talk Back to Your Brain Script you can read to yourself whenever your brain tries to make you feel guilty about practicing Self-Care.

Write it in words that are meaningful and convincing to you and your brain.

Think about what your brain might fear to cause it to make you feel guilty about Self-Care (you won't get stuff done, other people will disapprove, etc.), and address that head-on in your script.

Here's one I've written for myself:

Dear Brain,

I applaud your persistence in making me feel guilty for taking time for myself. Brilliant effort, but the only thing it accomplishes is making me feel like crap. And I know you don't want me to feel like crap. You're just afraid that I have a lot to do and that people I love might get upset with me if I do something just for me.

But they won't, truly. When I take care of myself, they feel the benefits because I share my good, uplifting energy with them. But when I don't, I get snappy and frustrated, and I bring a dark cloud with me. I bring everyone down and stress them out.

So, no one will be mad at me for taking care of myself. And when I have more energy, I get a lot more done, so you don't need to freak out about my to-do list. Seriously.

Lovingly but firmly,

Nataly

Stop Saying You Don't Have Time

One down—guilt—one to go—time! Not having enough time is the other reason I hear all the time for why someone doesn't practice Self-Care.

"I have too much work to get done, so I can't take time for myself right now."

"I'm exhausted, and I know I should take a break, but there are still dishes to be put away and the kitchen to clean and all this stuff I need to get done, so I can't do it."

I hear you. Life is busy, and there are endless to-dos and responsibilities pulling on you.

But saying you know you're tired but you can't take a break because there's stuff to do is like saying: *My car is low on fuel, but I can't stop for gas because I need to keep driving.*

You can't get the things done, or done well and in a sustainable way, without having enough emotional, mental, and physical energy to do them. And I absolutely refuse to accept that you can't find a little bit of time each day to fuel your energy.

You can find ten minutes in your day to practice Self-Care.

You can cut out ten minutes of social media scrolling. Ten minutes of reading the news. Ten minutes of sending an email that can wait until tomorrow (or maybe doesn't need to be sent?). Ten minutes of perfectly cleaning your kitchen. Ten minutes of making that gourmet dinner for your family.

We all have ten minutes, and ten minutes is all you need to begin to practice Self-Care daily.

It's not a matter of time. *It's a matter of making it a priority.*

When you say, *"I don't have time for Self-Care,"* what you really mean is "my Self-Care and filling my energy reservoir are not priorities for me."

Part of your challenge this week is to make your Self-Care a priority, even on the busiest of days, and to practice the Daily Fuel-Up.

PRACTICE

Daily Fuel-Up

Step 1: Make a list of as many things as you can think of that you can realistically do in ten minutes a day that help to fuel your emotional, mental, and physical energy.

Ask yourself: *Does doing this fuel my energy? Help me destress and relax? Does it feel restful?* If the answer is yes, it goes on the list!

I strongly encourage you to put a walk outside on your list. (Research shows a five-to-ten-minute walk outside boosts your mood and energy.)

If things come to mind that take longer than ten minutes, include them as well for those days when you have a bit more time.

Keep this list somewhere easy to find, so if you're ever stumped about what to do for your Daily Fuel-Up, it's there to remind you.

Step 2: Every day, schedule a Daily Fuel-Up on your calendar.

You can call it Hanging Out with a Pink Elephant for all I care—just as long as it makes it onto your calendar.

You don't have to do your Daily Fuel-Up at the same time every day. In fact, don't create more stress for yourself by being inflexible. The night before or in the morning, look at your schedule for the day and find the best time you can make it work.

Start with one Daily Fuel-Up, and if you feel you can fit in another, awesome. But one is great!

Step 3: When the time comes for your Daily Fuel-Up, DO IT.

Check in on your energy reservoir: *How's your emotional, mental, physical energy?* This will help you figure out what you could do to refuel.

You might be tempted to skip your Daily Fuel-Up, especially if you're busy. Your brain will have many excuses and reasons ready. DO NOT BUDGE. This is the time to Talk Back to Your Brain!

If for some reason you can't do your Daily Fuel-Up at that time, find a new time on the same day and move the time on your calendar.

Rest Is Not Doing Nothing

We can't talk about Self-Care without focusing on the four-letter word that's become like some forbidden activity in our get-more-done-always-be-doing world: *rest.*

I mentioned that I kept a daily journal during my first year of healing from burnout—here's one of the entries I wrote, about a month into it:

Woke up completely exhausted, but up. Groggy and went for a super-slow walk. Somehow made it to yoga, which was a struggle, but I did it.

Then I did what I have NEVER done:

Came home, got back into bed, and went to sleep. I was so groggy I didn't really think about what I was doing or how odd this was for me. I woke up to the alarm I set on my phone an hour later, shocked that I slept—I don't nap, I am the person who doesn't nap!—and feeling the flood of ALL the feelings of guilt, and OMG, THIS IS THE BEGINNING OF SOME NEW PHASE OF THE STORM WHERE I WILL JUST BE SLEEPING TO HIDE FROM MYSELF! I DON'T DESERVE TO SLEEP! WHY DO I DESERVE TO NAP NOW, WHAT A WASTE OF TIME!

NOTE TO SELF

Rest is the opposite of doing nothing.

I was literally in a panic because I took a break to rest! I'd always thought of rest as a waste of time, and I definitely didn't have time to do "nothing." But here's the thing:

Rest is the opposite of doing nothing!

When you take a break and do something that doesn't require focused thinking and analyzing, the frontal cortex, the part of your brain responsible for cognitive functions, gets to relax a bit. But while it's relaxing, a group of brain regions called the default modal network becomes more active. Your default network is responsible for tasks like organizing and processing information, making unexpected connections between concepts, and coming up with creative ideas. This is the reason we come up with ideas in the shower: taking a shower doesn't require a lot of mental work, so our frontal cortex gets to chill out, allowing the default modal network to get active and do its awesome thing.

Here's the punch line: your default network is most active when you're not engaged in challenging mental tasks. So when you take a break, you're not doing nothing. The default modal network in your brain is very busy and productive!

But wait, there's more!

Taking breaks to rest also helps to increase your focus and productivity. Most of our brains need a break every ninety minutes or so, and if we don't take it, our ability to focus and get stuff done suffers. Taking a break is an investment in our productivity, not something that detracts from it.

Studies in the workplace have shown, for example, that employees who take a break every ninety minutes report a 30 percent greater level of focus and 50 percent increased capacity to think creatively than those who don't take breaks or take just one during the day. Taking a break has also been shown to increase motivation because it allows you to step away and gain a fresh perspective on what you're doing.

So, the next time your brain tries to sabotage your Daily Fuel-Up or tell you that you don't have time to rest because you're too busy to do nothing, I want you to remember this research and talk back to your brain!

Don't Deny Yourself Joy (You Don't Have to Earn It)

A moment of truth: one of the Self-Care practices I've struggled the most to embrace is doing something that brings me joy *without it having any other productive or useful outcome.*

I love bold colors, crazy rings, and clothes with an edge to them. I wear bright yellow outfits when I speak and pair them with sparkly sneakers or two mismatched neon yellow and pink ones. It brings me joy, and I love seeing how it brings other people joy. (When was the last time you saw a speaker run out on stage wearing neon yellow everything? That's joy, right there.)

But for most of my life, I denied myself the joy of wearing stuff that made me happy. I made up a story that this was about money: "Cool clothes cost money, and I don't want to waste money on silly stuff like that." This story worked well because as a refugee, I've always had a fear of running out of money, even after working at well-paying jobs for decades. It also fit nicely with my bigger story about life being a struggle—I denied myself this little joy and that confirmed to me that there was little joy in life.

But my story was total BS because it doesn't take a lot of money to find clothes that make you happy or fun and colorful costume jewelry I now love so much. My story about money was a distraction. *I simply didn't feel that I deserved to experience joy.* I hadn't done enough to earn it.

What story is your brain using to convince you to deny yourself joy?

Is there a number on the scale you need to hit before you can buy yourself a fun new outfit?

Does your house need to be perfectly cleaned before you can sit down and drink some tea while you read a book?

Are you not supposed to "waste time" on doing stuff that brings you joy unless you've checked off every single thing from your mile-long to-do list?

Does everyone around you need to feel good before you give yourself permission to do something that brings you joy?

Take a moment and get honest about your joy denial story. Does denying yourself joy help you be a more Awesome Human, colleague, leader, parent, or friend?

No. Because joy isn't frivolous or extra. It's an essential, meaningful, and important part of the human experience and precious energy fuel that keeps you going and helps you to do difficult things and stuff you just really don't want to do but you know your future self would benefit from it. Here's a story to inspire you:

Carla is another awesome leader who participated in our Elevating Women Leaders program. She told me she had struggled to lose weight for the previous few years, after her divorce.

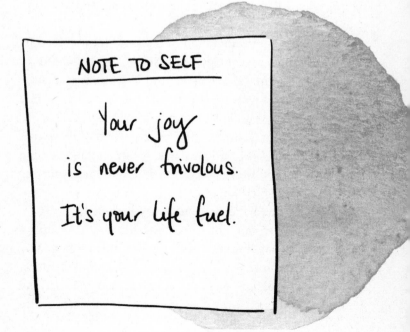

NOTE TO SELF

Your joy
is never frivolous.
It's your life fuel.

As a single mom running her own business, Carla would have had trouble making time to work out or cook healthy meals, I assumed, but that wasn't the case.

"I stick to my workouts during the week, I stick to my healthy eating, and then, after a few days, I sabotage all my efforts and eat too much junk food. I hate that I do that," Carla told me, frustrated.

I asked her if there was anything she enjoyed about her workouts. She said, "Not really." I asked her if some of the healthy foods she was so focused on eating brought her joy. She said no.

"You need to add joy," I told her.

"You're relying purely on your willpower to get through your workouts and eat healthy, and then your willpower runs out. Our willpower is not an unlimited resource, and it runs short especially when we're stressed and tired, something you experience often because your life is so busy. You need to stop treating yourself like a robot and add joy to your workouts and your food choices."

I told Carla about temptation bundling, a term coined by Amy Milkman, a psychology professor at the University of Pennsylvania. Temptation bundling works by linking an activity you want to do with an activity you need to do. By adding joy to something you need to do but don't really feel like doing, you help your brain to think more positively about that activity, which makes it easier to stick to. Temptation bundling builds a bridge between your current and future self: your current self gets to enjoy something, and your future self gets to benefit from your having done what you need to do.

I asked Carla to think of something she could do during her workout that brought her joy, and she immediately came up with the answer: essential oils. She worked out on her elliptical machine at home, and she decided that she would diffuse her favorite essential oils only while she worked out. Carla also committed to finding some healthy foods she actually enjoyed.

A few weeks after we spoke, Carla wrote me an excited email to say that for the first time in ages she had lost weight, she felt great, and her workouts and healthy eating were actually more enjoyable! It's been almost a year, and she has continued to get into better shape—and she credits temptation bundling and adding joy to her food and working out as her biggest helpers.

This week, I challenge you to practice your joy as part of your Self-Care and, specifically, to practice temptation bundling by making something you need to do more enjoyable.

PRACTICE

Create Your Temptation Bundle

Step 1: Pick your need-to-do activity.

Think of something you'd like to do regularly but don't enjoy or have trouble sticking to. Working out? Organizing your desk? Reading more?

Step 2: Pick your want-to-do activity.

Think of something you could do during your need-to-do activity that would help it feel more enjoyable. Maybe you watch your favorite Netflix show only while you work out or sit in your favorite chair at home only while you read.

Step 3: Get exclusive.

Temptation bundling works best if you do your want-to-do activity *only* while you do your need-to-do one. That means you watch the Netflix show you love *only* while you're working out, and you sit in your favorite chair *only* while you're reading. You want your brain to associate the specific want-to-do activity with the specific need-to-do activity, so keep the two exclusive to each other.

Learning New Things = Self-Care (and Helps Prevent Burnout)

I want to do a shoutout for learning as an awesome form of Self-Care that doesn't get the oomph it deserves. Learning new things has tons of mental health benefits:

- The process of learning stimulates new brain-cell growth and can slow aging and neurodegenerative diseases like Alzheimer's.

- Learning something that's a bit challenging and slightly outside of your comfort zone puts you in a state known as *flow*, which gives you a sense of fulfillment and enjoyment.

- Learning how to do something gives you a sense of mastery and progress, and it helps you feel more confident about accomplishing bigger things and reaching meaningful goals.

There's another huge benefit of making time to learn new things: it helps you develop interests and have a richer, fuller life outside of work. One of the main causes of burnout is overidentifying with your work and, boy, does that one ring true for me. For most of my career, and especially when I founded my own company, so much of my worth was tied up in my work. Work stress, work to-dos, work achievements, and work failures were the main players in my life and determined how I felt. Basically, I *was* my work.

I've always wanted to paint, but it was only after I burned out that I let myself do it. It had always felt like an indulgence that had nothing to do with my career success or taking care of my family, so my brain judged it not worthy. But allowing myself to learn a new skill just because it brought me joy was magical and healing.

I've fallen in love with painting! And one of the biggest lessons I learned after allowing myself to dive into it is how healing it was not only for me but also for everyone around me. Making art makes me happy. It refreshes me, enriches me, and helps me embrace my Awesome Human. Every single person around me feels the benefits of that. Sure, my family loves seeing my art on our walls, and people who attend virtual talks I do from home enjoy seeing it behind me, but the biggest benefit to them is my energy fueled by doing and learning something fun.

This week, I encourage you to commit to learning something new as part of practicing Self-Care. It can be anything you want—there are no right or wrong things to learn! If something interests you, you're curious about it, or it brings you joy, go for it! Start small, maybe ten to fifteen minutes a day, and you can use some of your Daily Fuel-Ups for learning new things.

Here are a few ideas:

- Pick up a new cookbook or find a new recipe online and give it a try.

- Try a new craft, like painting, drawing, collaging, or sewing.

- Begin learning a new skill, like photography, wood carving, or writing.

- Consider signing up for a course, perhaps online if that's easier to manage.

- Read about people you admire—your favorite artists, authors, or designers.

Enjoy your learning, and do it because you want to learn, grow, and explore something new, not because it's something you "should do" or need to do. It's such a beautiful, natural, and expansive part of the human experience, and I'm really excited for you to make it a priority for yourself.

Practices in This Chapter

Lens of Self-Care
No/Yes Trade-Off
Write a No-Guilt, Self-Care, Talk Back to Your Brain Script
Daily Fuel-Up
Create Your Temptation Bundle

Your Note to Self

What is something you want to remember, practice, or reflect on from this chapter?

AWESOME HUMAN AWARD

I hope you feel fueled and energized after this week and like you've been a really good friend to yourself. It takes your inner warrior to talk back to your brain and bust through the guilt to make Self-Care a priority, so you've definitely earned the **No-Guilt Self-Care Warrior** award!

CHAPTER 12

Week 4—Intentional Kindness

This week you're going to become a Kindness Champion, and I'm really excited for you. It might sound weird to talk about kindness as a skill, but it's such a powerful mindset shift to make.

I'll admit it: I didn't make this mindset shift intentionally—my burnout forced me into it.

I'd always thought of myself as a generally kind person. I made a big deal out of family members' and friends' birthdays with surprises and creative gifts, went out of my way to find the face powder my grandma liked and the shirts with holes for cufflinks my grandpa wanted, and made elaborate gourmet meals for my husband and daughter almost daily. Oh, and I worried *a lot* about people I cared about, which somehow always felt like an act of kindness, although it seems odd in retrospect. But to me, worrying was caring.

Kindness, for my earlier self, was about grand gestures and sacrifice. It wasn't something I'd made a priority in my regular daily interactions with other people. Instead of random acts of kindness, I practiced very special big acts of kindness. It wasn't until the universe hit me over the head with a two-by-four and

I completely burned out that I realized what I'd always prioritized above kindness: efficiency.

I was that person in Starbucks who had her credit card out and pointed the right way to go into the credit card reader before I even got close to the register. I'd tell the barista my order, which I made sure was clear and succinct, and when my latte was ready, I would grab it with a quick "Thanks!" as I was walking away. At work, I loved getting right to it during meetings and thought the whole idea of "watercooler chit-chat" was silly and a waste of time.

I approached my days like a series of sprints I had to finish as efficiently as possible. Who had time to stop and chat with a colleague or actually look at the barista handing me my coffee and say, "Thank you"? Not busy people like me.

Don't get me wrong: I wasn't rude, and it's not like I never said "Thank you" to people. It's that I saw no purpose in small, kind interactions with others, especially people I didn't know, so I viewed them as extra and unnecessary, space fillers between productive activities. This reflected my general approach to life: everything I did had to help me accomplish something and be productive. The more I could shrink the time between one to-do and another, the better.

When I completely burned out, I couldn't sprint through my days anymore. My efficiency became useless because I could hardly function, so getting a lot done was out of the question. Suddenly, there were time and space in my days, which scared the daylights out of me but also created room for kindness.

At first, this was completely unintentional. I'd go to a café, and because I didn't have the energy to be my usual ultra-efficient self, I would move more slowly. I found myself actually saying hello to the person behind the counter, noticing that she was wearing funky earrings, and telling her that I liked them. I'd smile and say "Hi" to the people in line behind me at the grocery store or rush to move my mat in my yoga class so the woman walking in late would have a spot. I began to make it a point every week to check in on family and friends, with no occasion required, and made more time to truly listen to what they shared rather than rushing toward some conclusion, like making a plan or fixing a problem.

NOTE TO SELF

Trade some efficiency for kindness.

I'd traded some of my efficiency for kindness and given myself an amazing gift: the gift of warmth and human connection. I didn't realize it at the time, but this was a big part of my healing from burnout and the go-go-go-always-run-faster-do-more way I had been living. Small, kind interactions with people—those I knew well or not at all—wove a supportive net around me. Rather than seeing these as a waste of time, I began to recognize how essential they were to my well-being and my joy!

Don't get me wrong: I still love efficiency and getting stuff done. I'm still that person who holds her credit card the right way at the coffee shop so I don't waste an extra second when I put it into the card reader. The difference now is that I love finding ways to connect with others, to say something kind or to help in a small way *as* I go about getting stuff done. These tiny moments of kindness and human connection have become part of my daily fuel—and I love the "inefficiency" they bring into my days. The entire fabric of my days has changed, and even on the toughest days, these kind interactions became like a soft buffer, helping me to feel just a little less awful.

What I've experienced is supported by research, including how a tiny, kind interaction with another person can improve your mood. In one study, researchers asked volunteers to go into a coffee shop. Members of one group were told to just order the way they usually do and the other to have one small, kind interaction with another person. The group that did the latter reported feeling more uplifted when they left the shop. Similar studies have been done in subways, including New York City subways, which, believe me, after I lived there for a decade, are not what you'd call uplifting places. Still, when experiment participants had one kind interaction with another person while riding the subway, they reported feeling happier and less stressed.

This is the power of Intentional Kindness, and your challenge this week is to find as many ways as possible to practice it: **to be intentionally kind toward others and not expect anything in return.**

Here's your focus practice for this week.

PRACTICE

Lens of Kindness

Look at your days this week through the Lens of Kindness to do something kind or helpful for someone else.

Remember that your acts of kindness can be tiny, and what matters is your intention to do something kind without expecting anything in return.

Have a little brainstorming session, and jot down a few acts of kindness you want to make sure to do during the week. (You can check them off as you do them and make your inner productivity lover happy, too!)

Pay attention to how you feel when you make kindness a priority, and use that as your fuel to commit to the practice of Intentional Kindness during this week and beyond.

Notice how "not expecting anything in return" is part of the Intentional Kindness definition. This can be tricky. Many people tell me they get frustrated and even resentful when they do something kind but the other person doesn't reciprocate. Even people who say they don't expect anything in return for their kindness, upon reflection, admit that they do expect the recipient to thank them. This was something I was stuck on for a long time, and sometimes I still catch myself anticipating a thank-you.

But in its purest, most genuine form, kindness is something you do *without any expectation of getting something back,* including a thank-you. Intentional Kindness asks us to practice it because we want to do it and it feels good to do it, nothing more.

My teacher told me once that we experience 100 percent of the emotions we give to others. When we do something kind, we feel kind. When we express anger, we feel angry.

Her point wasn't that we should never express our frustration or anger toward someone, but rather, we should be aware of how what we express toward others affects our own emotional and mental energy. When you do something kind, you fuel yourself with a sense of connection. That's your reward.

Researchers have done experiments to show that different centers in your brain light up when you do something just to be kind or because you're expecting something in return. The results showed that *your brain rewards only genuine kindness without expectations.*

Kindness turns out to be a selfless selfish act. No, that's not a typo. Kindness helps you feel less alone and more connected and uplifted . . . but only if you practice it without expecting to get anything in return.

The Power of Human Connection

We are not meant to go through life alone. A sense of human connection and belonging (to family, community, society) is a core human need. To survive, we need to cooperate with other people, and no one will cooperate with you if you're not kind or helpful to them in some way.

In fact, a sense of human connection is so essential that our brains interpret feeling isolated as danger. Studies have shown that when people feel isolated, they have higher levels of inflammation. Inflammation is your body's process of fighting things that harm it—like infections and injuries. Think about that! (By the way, just for clarity: feeling isolated and spending time alone are totally different things. We all need some alone time to decompress, and some of us—raising my hand—might need more than others. But when we don't feel connected to other people, we feel isolated.)

To encourage you to connect with others, your brain rewards you every time you do something helpful or kind. It releases oxytocin—known as a *hug hormone* because we release it when we hug each other—and serotonin—a neurotransmitter—both of which make you feel good. What's awesome is that this good feeling isn't just yours: the recipient of your act of kindness feels it, and even someone observing an act of kindness gets a feel-good boost. If you remember just how contagious human emotions are, this won't surprise you.

> **NOTE TO SELF**
>
> The most meaningful happiness comes from being kind and helpful to someone else.

But will it surprise you to know that the person who feels the biggest hit of good fuel from an act of kindness is the person doing it? It's true: in many studies, people who performed kind and helpful acts at work reported feeling happier and more satisfied with their jobs than the recipients of their kindness did.

Speaking of work, I need to do a shoutout: yes, kindness belongs at work, and if you work, part of your challenge this week is to find opportunities to practice Intentional Kindness with your colleagues. Here are a few really simple ideas and a reminder that what makes your acts of kindness most meaningful is your intention to connect, support, or elevate the other person in some way.

Small Acts of Kindness at Work

Check in with colleagues	Ask colleagues how they are doing; don't make it about work; and most importantly, LISTEN to what they have to say. Don't interrupt; don't make this about yourself or jump in with advice. Just connect, one Awesome Human to another. (If you're the boss, doing this regularly is one of the best ways to show your team members that you care about them as people, not just employees.)
Practice gratitude	Express your gratitude to your colleagues, and make sure to tell them *why* you are grateful for them. Sharing your gratitude is an awesome way to practice kindness.
Surprise with small gifts	Surprise a colleague with her favorite cup of coffee or a book on a topic she might be interested in. Bonus points for homemade treats!

Doing something kind not only makes you feel good but also acts as a stress buffer. Researchers have found that people who engaged in more helpful behavior showed a lower increase in negative emotions in response to high daily stress and reported no dampening of their well-being. I absolutely experienced this when I made Intentional Kindness a daily priority.

Here's a practice to try when you're having a low moment or a tough day.

PRACTICE

Blast Your Stress with Kindness

When you feel stressed, overwhelmed, or anxious: pause, acknowledge your feelings, and come up with a few acts of kindness you can do.

This can be as simple as texting a friend or walking over to a colleague to check in. You can also combine your Gratitude and Intentional Kindness practices by sending an email, text, or note to someone you appreciate and telling them why.

It's important to do a few acts of kindness close together to help your brain shift out of the stress spiral and feel the most positive effect. There's no formula or magic number, but I love the number three, so if it's helpful, aim for that.

The Kindness Boomerang

There's no "give one, take one" in kindness, no "I did something kind, so you need to do something kind for me." But kindness *is* a boomerang that will come back to you, sometimes in unexpected ways.

I got to experience this a few winters ago, when a snowstorm almost made me miss a speaking engagement. My morning flight from Boston to San Jose was cancelled, and there were no seats available on other flights when I checked online. I was supposed to be onstage in front of thousands of people the next morning, and I was very much freaking out.

Not really sure what they could do, I decided to call JetBlue customer support anyway. When the agent picked up the call and said, "How can I help you?" I asked her how she was holding up because the storm was definitely causing chaos.

"Wow, thank you for asking," she said, surprised. "I'm not used to customers asking me how I'm doing. To be honest, it's been a really stressful day."

We chatted for a minute or two—about our mutual dislike of the snow and our kids' love of it—before I told her about my dilemma.

"Let me talk to my manager and see what I can do," she told me. She took my number and said she would call me back as soon as she could.

Twenty minutes later, she and her manager had found me a seat on the last flight out that night. I was so grateful! As I waited at the airport later that evening, the agent texted me to say that she had checked, and the plane would depart on time. And when I landed in San Jose, the first text I saw was from her, saying, "Welcome to San Jose! I hope you had a good flight and got some sleep before your talk!"

I was so touched by her kindness. Although I'm certain she would have gone out of her way to help me anyway, I'd like to think that my pausing to connect to her as a human being and ask her how she was played a small part. My tiny act of kindness came back to me like a boomerang.

Your kindness boomerang will come back to you, and the more boomerangs you launch by doing something kind, the more kindness will swirl around you and support you.

How Listening Can Move Mountains

One of the things I discovered when I stopped thinking of kindness in terms of big and bold acts was how much power there is in simply listening to the other person. It's one of the kindest things we can do for each other, yet few of us think of it that way.

I used to suck at listening. It's definitely still a work in progress, and my brain looooves to run ahead as someone is talking, ready with a response or suggestion. I know I'm not alone in this: most of us don't listen to *listen*, we listen to *respond*.

We ask someone how they are doing, and as the person is talking, our brain starts to think of what we're going to say when they are done, which often involves sharing advice or relating our own similar experience. Our brain is like an impatient child who just can't wait to get a word in edgewise.

But this isn't really listening. It's more like information exchange. If you're busy thinking about your response, you're not truly present and attentive. I read that hostage negotiators work in teams, but the only person talking is the lead negotiator—the others just focus on listening so they don't miss a single thing. You're also not truly present and attentive if you're going over your to-do list in your head or endlessly glancing at your phone. And yet, the true gift of listening *is* your full attention and presence!

Think about how great it feels when people really listen to you, without interrupting, trying to fix your problem, giving advice, jumping ahead, or making you feel they would rather be doing something else. You feel cared for, acknowledged, and truly seen, which fulfills your need of belonging and connection. This is the true gift of listening as an act of kindness: it helps both you and the person you're listening to experience that feeling of belonging. Like other acts of kindness, it's a boomerang that comes back to you.

Listening is an act of kindness that has more power than you might recognize.

One of my favorite stories about Wayne Dyer, author of more than forty books, spiritual teacher, and someone whose work has influenced a lot of my own, is about how his listening led to a publishing contract, although not at all in the way you would expect.

Dyer was looking for a publisher for his first book, *Your Erroneous Zones*. His agent was able to set up a meeting with a senior editor at a top publishing house, a really big deal. When Dyer showed up to the meeting, he noticed that the editor was tense and preoccupied with something. So instead of launching into talking about his book, he asked if there was anything he could do to help. The two men ended up talking for the duration of the meeting about some difficult personal challenges the editor had been facing. Dyer listened, gave him his full attention, and never brought up his book.

When Dyer's agent heard about what happened, he told him that he had wasted an important meeting, and now his book's chances of getting published were slim. But a few days later, the agent got a call from the editor Dyer had met. The editor said he didn't know anything about the book but he wanted to work with someone like Dyer, who clearly cared deeply about helping people. *Your Erroneous Zones* ended up becoming one of the top-selling books of all time, with an estimated one hundred million copies in print.

I love this story so much! When Dyer noticed that the editor seemed tense, he first practiced Acceptance: he witnessed the situation as it was ("the editor seems really tense and distracted") versus how his brain thought it "should have been" ("the editor *should* be excited to hear about my book!"). His next best step was to practice Intentional Kindness: he asked the editor if he wanted to share what was on his mind, and he listened.

By shifting his attention from his own agenda to doing something kind, Dyer helped the editor feel less alone, and the two men were able to connect on a deep human level, not just as a writer and editor. They built trust, and the editor got to know the kind of person Dyer was—as important as, if not more important than, hearing about his book.

What Dyer practiced in that meeting was more than just kind listening—he also practiced compassion.

The Lens of Compassion

Compassion means you recognize that other people might be struggling with something, and you want to alleviate their struggle in some way. During his meeting, Dyer recognized that the editor was upset and offered to help by listening.

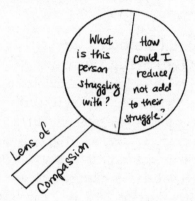

If this definition of compassion sounds familiar, awesome, you've been paying attention! We already talked about it in chapter 5, on self-compassion. Self-compassion has the same two components, just applied toward yourself: understanding that you're a human being who struggles and doing something to alleviate your struggle.

Let's jump back to our Tense Boss scenario. What if, when you realized your boss was not smiling and seemed tense, you'd put your brain's dramatic stories about getting fired aside and practiced Compassion? It could go something like this:

Acceptance: *My boss seems tense. What is the next best thing I could do?*

Lens of Compassion: *Maybe something else is stressing her out. I'll ask how she is doing and see if there's anything I can do to help.*

By combining Acceptance with Compassion, you would have shifted your attention away from ruminating on how upset your boss must be with your work and used it to perform an act of kindness by listening and maybe even identifying a way to help. Imagine how much your boss would appreciate your doing this and how much less stress and anxiety you would experience! Less wasting of energy on being worried about being fired, more using that energy to do something valuable and helpful.

How Compassion Helps to Reduce Your Own Struggle

It's definitely easier to practice Compassion in some situations than in others. When someone is rude or disrespectful to you, Compassion might be the furthest from your mind. Believe me, my natural reaction fuse is a short one, so I know from firsthand experience that what I want to do in those situations is lash out and say something rude back, not practice Compassion!

But tell me this: how does snapping back at someone actually make you feel? Okay, right in the heat of the moment, probably pretty good—you get a hit of satisfaction of getting back at the person. *Aha! She was rude to me, so now I've taught her a lesson of what it feels like!* But after that initial reaction, how do you feel? In my case, usually crappy. I tend to replay the exchange that just happened, get more and more frustrated over what the person did, and then get annoyed at myself for reacting the way I did. I drain my emotional energy and cause myself more struggle.

Not helpful. This is why I'm going to suggest a different approach: when someone does something that annoys or frustrates you, use the Lens of Compassion.

Yes, really.

Pause and consider that the reason for people's behavior might have nothing to do with you. Their rudeness, although it feels bad, isn't personal, and they are acting this way because they are struggling with something—they just got yelled at by their boss, they are worried about a sick relative, their dog peed on the floor as they had to rush out to work, you name it. They are not horrible humans out to get you and make you feel awful. They are human beings just like you, dealing with life and juggling many struggles and challenges.

Did the voice in your head just go: *But why should I let them off the hook?* I hear you. Mine does that, too.

So, here's the answer:

Compassion is not about letting anyone off the hook or tolerating bad behavior without ever saying a word. I'm asking you to practice Compassion to protect your energy by shifting your attention from how other people's actions upset *you* to considering that *they* might be struggling with something and identifying one way you could help.

Sometimes helping is listening. Sometimes helping is not reacting with anger right away. Sometimes it's saying a supportive word or two. Regardless of the action you take, practicing Compassion means taking your attention away from how people's actions offended *you* to *their* struggles. When you make this shift, you'll notice that you actually feel less upset.

That's right: *Reacting with Compassion helps you first.* When you react with Compassion instead of lashing out at people, you protect your well-being and avoid wasting your energy on feeling upset, offended, or angry. Studies have linked Compassion with lower blood pressure, improved immune system, reduced stress and depression, and speedier recovery from an illness. Like other forms of kindness, Compassion creates a sense of human connection, which doesn't just feel good but is good for you.

NOTE TO SELF

Practicing compassion is an awesome way to take things less personally (And stress less!)

Compassion toward others also helps you to understand yourself better and treat yourself with greater Compassion. The more you practice recognizing other people's struggles and allowing room for them to make mistakes and be imperfect, the better you become at approaching yourself in a similar way. The more I've practiced Kindness and Compassion toward others, the easier it's been to practice it toward myself.

Now that I've given you my pep talk on why Compassion rocks, here's how to use the Lens of Compassion when someone's actions upset, frustrate, or annoy you.

PRACTICE

Lens of Compassion for Frustration

When someone does something rude or frustrating, pause and practice the two steps of the Lens of Compassion:

Step 1: Put yourself in the other person's shoes.

What might have happened to them earlier in the day to cause them pain, stress, or struggle? How might that influence why they are acting this way?

Feel free to make up a story about something the person might be struggling with! It doesn't have to be true, but creating the story in your mind will help you to step into compassion and reduce your own feelings of stress.

Step 2: Identify one way you could reduce the person's struggle.

Most often, the way you can reduce people's struggle after they are rude toward you is by not responding with anger, which would just pile on to their struggle.

I recognize that your brain might really hate even the idea of this practice. Shouldn't you express your feelings and set the person right? Yes, sometimes that's important to do, especially if this person is someone you know. But when people are upset or struggling, do you think they are open to hearing about how you feel? And when you're upset, can you really communicate your feelings in the clearest way?

The honest answer to both of these questions is no. This is why I am asking you to first practice the Lens of Compassion, so you can avoid wasting your emotional and mental energy and get to a calmer, less reactive place.

Here's a Talk Back to Your Brain Script for those times when your brain is really stubborn and doesn't want to go anywhere near the Compassion:

Dear Brain,

I recognize that you're really upset by what this person did, and you want to tell them all the ways in which they hurt you. Your feelings are valid, and you have the right to feel what you feel.

But lashing out right this minute will only make things worse. You are not thinking straight, and more importantly, it will only waste energy and make you more upset.

Instead, let's just consider that this other person is not evil and didn't do this for the sole purpose of making you upset. Maybe they had a really bad, no-good, terrible day. Maybe something difficult is happening in their life that's causing them not to be at their best. You know how you get when things are tough, right?

So what can you do not to pile more struggle onto this person? Well, maybe for now, not saying anything back is a really great idea. Not forever, but just for now.

Give them a chance to cool off and hopefully resolve whatever they are dealing with, and then you can have a calmer conversation about how what they did affected you. Or maybe by that point you'll forget all about it.

With love,

Me

AWESOME HUMAN AWARD

Making the choice to practice Compassion instead of snapping back at someone who does something rude or upsetting is an advanced practice, so after you've done it even once, you've definitely earned the **Could Have Snapped but Chose Compassion Instead** award!

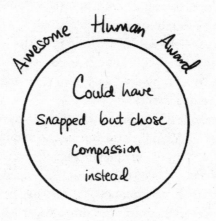

How Compassion Can Make Difficult Conversations Easier

If I think about some of the most anxiety-filled times in my life, many involved having difficult conversations.

A boy breaking up with me in high school (ouch!)

Getting some tough feedback during my review at my first job (I still remember it)

Having to fire someone on my team (one of the hardest things ever to do)

Often, the anticipation of a difficult conversation is just as stressful, or more so, than the actual talk. Although you can't hide from life and avoid having tough conversations, there *is* a way to struggle less through them by practicing Intentional Kindness and Compassion.

A few months ago, I got an email from Kelly, my speaking agent for several years. She asked if we could chat because she had an update for me. Kelly and her team were instrumental in helping to launch my speaking career, so naturally my brain immediately freaked out. *OMG, she is leaving the firm, and what's going to happen to ME, who is going to represent ME, what am I going to do?!*

Kelly was my last call of the day on a busy Friday after a really busy week, and I was really dreading it. I realized that if I was right and she was leaving the firm, she was probably not looking forward to this call, either. So I decided to practice Compassion by shifting my focus from *How does this affect me?* to *How could I support her?*

I was right: Kelly was leaving the firm. She was making a big career change and joining a startup. As she told me about it, I could sense so many of her different feelings, from excitement to doubt. Because I'd been part of many startups before, I gave her some words of reassurance and told her how grateful I was for her commitment to me through my early speaking years. I could literally feel her exhale a little bit, and that made me feel awesome!

Given her departure and other changes at the firm, it became clear that I would need to find a new speaking agent. This was a stressful realization. For someone who makes a large part of their business income from speaking, having a great agent is essential. Would I be able to find someone awesome? Would that awesome agent want to work with me? Kelly was ready with a few recommendations we chatted about, and she offered to introduce me to them. By the end of our call, we had a little plan of action.

When I got off the phone, I felt a mix of emotions: I was overwhelmed with the change coming, excited and nervous about finding a new agent, and grateful for Kelly's commitment to guide me through the transition. But it also felt really good to have supported Kelly.

Later that evening, she sent me the most heartfelt email, with a subject line that read: "Thank you for your kindness." She told me she had been dreading our call and feeling anxious about it, and she was grateful to me for making the conversation so easy.

Practicing Compassion during our call didn't eliminate my challenge of having to find a new speaking agent or eliminate my sadness over not working with Kelly anymore. But Compassion reduced my internal struggle by shifting my thoughts away from stressing about an outcome I couldn't control and toward ways I could support and help Kelly. (Oh, and if you're curious, I signed with a great new agent a few months later, the first one Kelly had recommended.)

I love all the science behind why being kind and compassionate feels good, but I think the main reason is both simpler and more profound: being kind taps into the best of ourselves, our Awesome Human core. No wonder research shows that when you do your work with Compassion, you're more effective, convincing, and trustworthy. Your practice of Intentional Kindness brings out your best and opens up the best in anyone on the receiving end of it.

I hope this feeling of operating from your Awesome Human core is a feeling you get to experience a LOT as you practice Intentional Kindness this week.

Practices in This Chapter

Lens of Kindness
Blast Your Stress with Kindness
Lens of Compassion for Frustration

Your Note to Self

What is something you want to remember, practice, or reflect on from this chapter?

AWESOME HUMAN AWARD

After you've done your practices and completed the week, proudly give yourself the **Kindness Champion** award! You've earned it and spread so much good while doing it!

CHAPTER 13

Week 5—The Bigger Why

You are now ready to dive into the fifth emotional fitness skill you're going to master: your Bigger Why. When it comes to strengthening your resilience, working through fear, and not only surviving but also growing and evolving through challenges, this is your can't-do-without skill. **The Bigger Why is the skill of regularly connecting with your sense of meaning and purpose by identifying how your daily activities and tasks support your bigger goals, help others, or contribute to something greater than yourself.**

A sense of meaning is one of those things you know when you feel it, but it can be difficult to describe. I remember thinking that meaning was something I needed to go out and find "somewhere out there." I didn't exactly know what it was, but I was sure I would know it when I found it—and that I hadn't yet. Many people tell me they struggle to find their meaning in life.

It's really difficult to feel that way. Just as we need to feel that we're not alone and we belong to something greater than ourselves, we need to feel that our lives have purpose. Having a sense of meaning is linked to greater emotional, mental, and physical well-being, with studies showing that it reduces stress and risk of depression and increases social connection and motivation.

So here's a promise: by the end of this week, you will experience a greater sense of meaning. Not only that, you will learn how to use your sense of meaning to help you do difficult things and move through fear. The reason I feel so confident about this is very simple: **your meaning and purpose aren't somewhere out there but right here, within your life as it is, right now.**

The first step is to know what you're looking for, so let's get super-specific about meaning and purpose. (Side note: I'm going to use *meaning* and *purpose* interchangeably, even though I am sure some psychologists would disapprove. But because I'm not writing a college psych textbook, I'm going to be a courageous rebel and do it.)

Here's how purpose is defined in psychology: *"A stable and generalized intention to accomplish something that is at once meaningful to the self and of consequence to the world beyond the self."*

I don't usually like big formal definitions of anything, but I share this one with you because I find it really helpful.

If you break it down, you'll see that meaning and purpose have three parts:

1. In contrast with simple day-to-day things, like working on a presentation at work or making dinner for your family, they are longer lasting (not just about what you're doing right now).

2. Meaning and purpose involve reaching in some way beyond yourself (contributing to another person, a team, a bigger goal).

3. They involve achievement, progress, or completion (you want to accomplish something).

To put it even more simply, meaning and purpose transcend *you* by impacting other people, and they transcend the *present moment and activity* by contributing to something longer lasting and bigger in scope.

The customer presentation you're working on has meaning because it will help your customer (someone outside of you) choose the best solution for their business (a far-reaching achievement). The dinner you're making will help your family (someone other than you) feel nourished and cared for (lasting positive impact).

I picked these two simple examples because on the surface, they might not seem that meaningful—they are just things you do as part of your day. But when you look more closely and apply the Lens of the Bigger Why, you realize that actually, there is purpose and meaning within them. Your meaning and purpose in life aren't "somewhere out there" but are hiding in plain sight in the activities you do every single day.

This week, your challenge is to use the Lens of the Bigger Why to uncover meaning and purpose within the things you're already doing. Here's your focus practice for the week.

PRACTICE

Lens of the Bigger Why

As you go through the week, begin to look at your daily activities through the Lens of the Bigger Why to uncover their meaning and purpose.

Ask yourself:

Who does this help? (my colleagues, my customers,
my family, etc.)

How does this contribute to a goal I'm working
toward? (e.g., becoming a better artist or writer,
getting into better shape, etc.)

How does this positively impact something outside
of myself? (e.g., it helps the environment, makes my
neighborhood more beautiful or safer, etc.)

Of course, I'm not asking you to do this for every single thing you do this week. (So please go ahead and brush your teeth just like you normally would.) But do it for a few tasks, especially if they are stressful or if you can't think of any possible way they could be meaningful.

Notice how you feel when you connect something you do to a greater sense of meaning and purpose. Do you feel a bit more motivated to do it? Do you feel like you have more energy to bring to it? Does the activity itself feel a little less daunting, stressful, or annoying?

How Practicing Your Bigger Why Can Make You Fall in Love with Your To-Do List

Now that I have your attention with this section title, please don't hold it over me. Maybe you won't fall in love with your to-do list, but I promise you that when you practice your Bigger Why, you'll dread it less, a really big win in my book.

A few years ago, I read about a research study that's become one of my favorite examples of how connecting what you do daily to your sense of meaning helps you to find more satisfaction and, dare I say it, more joy in even the most mundane parts of your work and life. It was conducted by Amy Wrzesniewski, a professor at the Yale School of Management who decided to understand what strategies janitors in a hospital system were using to find satisfaction in their low-paid, low-skill jobs.

What she found was remarkable: janitors who had the highest job satisfaction talked about their work by focusing on the why (their purpose) instead of the what (the tasks they had to do every day). When asked what they did for work, they didn't say things like, "I take out the garbage and clean the floors." Instead, they talked about how they helped patients get better or helped their family members who visited them feel a little more comfortable.

Think about that! Simply by connecting their mundane work tasks to how they contributed and helped someone else, the janitors were happier and more satisfied with their jobs.

What's more, these janitors expanded the scope of their jobs. One went out of the way to find out if the patient was allergic to any chemicals to avoid using them while cleaning the patient's room. Another kept track of which patients had fewer visitors and made sure to double back and visit that patient twice during their shift.

Researchers called this "job crafting"—the janitors were crafting jobs they wanted to do out of the jobs they had to do. And they did this by adding elements that brought them a greater sense of meaning by being kind and compassionate toward others.

This is the power of the Bigger Why: when you practice connecting how what you do contributes to something greater than yourself, you find more satisfaction within your daily activities, and you become fueled and motivated to do more things that bring you meaning.

Let's talk about motivation for a moment, shall we?

When you're feeling overwhelmed or your energy is depleted, getting motivated can be tough. I've never had a problem with motivation until I burned out—and then suddenly, I couldn't find a drop of it.

So if you're having trouble getting motivated, the first thing I want you to do is check in with yourself and your energy reservoir. If you're exhausted, hungry, or sleep deprived or have been pushing yourself to the limit, you need to fuel your energy before you can worry about getting motivated. You can't just will yourself to do it.

> ## NOTE TO SELF
>
> Look at your to-do list through the lens of "how can I contribute?" vs. "stuff I have to do"

But after you've done that, the next best way to boost motivation is to practice your Bigger Why and identify how what you need to do contributes to something other than yourself or helps you work toward a goal that's meaningful to you.

During a workshop at a tech company where we practiced doing this, I asked if anyone would share how it went. A woman named Jen, responsible for one of the product teams, raised her hand and said:

"There's a report I need to put together every week summarizing what our team worked on so that we can share it with other teams, like sales and marketing. I usually dread doing it. I need to bug people on my team to share info with me and then put it all together—it's not my favorite thing to do. But now that I've thought about my Bigger Why for doing this report, I realize it helps the other teams we work with, helps my team members because their work is recognized, and ultimately, I guess it even helps our customers because when the teams communicate better our product is better."

She actually began to smile as she talked: "While I can't say that now I'm ecstatic to do it, my mindset has shifted. I dread it less and feel more motivated to get it done."

By using the Lens of the Bigger Why, Jen was able to see how doing her weekly report helped others (her team, other teams, the company's customers), and this fueled her with more motivation to get it done.

Here's an awesome practice to put this in action.

PRACTICE

To-Do List Makeover

Look at your to-do list and focus on the tasks that you don't feel like doing. You know those tasks you keep writing on your to-do list every day and then just moving to the next day, and the next, and the next? They make great candidates for this practice.

Use the Lens of the Bigger Why and ask yourself: *Who does this help? How does this contribute to something in a positive way?*

After you have the answer, reframe that task through the Lens of the Bigger Why. Here are a few examples of how this might work:

To-Do	With Bigger Why Lens
Finish presentation for a client meeting	Finish this presentation, which will help our team do a better job explaining our solution to the client and help the client make the best choice for their business
Cook dinner	Cook dinner for my family to keep them fueled and healthy and to give us a chance to spend some quality time together
Write an email to my old boss asking for a reference for a new job I'm applying for	Write an email to my old boss asking for a reference for a new job because it can really help my chances of getting it and help me grow into the next phase of my career

AWESOME HUMAN AWARD

Our ever-growing to-do lists can be a huge source of stress, so after you've done this practice a few times, you definitely deserve the **Finding More Meaning and Less Dread on My To-Do List** award!

Bigger Why as Your Bridge of Resilience

Now I get to tell you about the real superpower of practicing your Bigger Why and how it can become your Bridge of Resilience through your toughest challenges. I don't think it's an exaggeration to say that I've been (somewhat patiently) holding my breath to wait for you to get to this part of your Awesome Human Project so I could share it with you!

For most of my life, I thought that to be resilient meant to be tough. It was part of the reason I never allowed myself to actually feel any difficult feelings—tough people wouldn't do that. But I had it wrong. Resilience has nothing to do with being tough or not feeling feelings. In fact, research shows that the most resilient people experience difficult feelings intensely as they go through traumatic life events and difficulties. But they fuel their resilience by finding positive meaning *within* life's challenges, which helps them not only get through them but also grow in meaningful ways.

Resilience is the ability to positively adapt amid adversity.

One of the people who has greatly influenced my work and, specifically, my thoughts on meaning and resilience is Viktor Frankl, a Holocaust survivor, psychiatrist, and the author of *Man's Search for Meaning*, one of the most powerful books I've ever read. In 1946, just after World War II, Frankl wrote about his time as a prisoner in a concentration camp and how he managed to survive the utmost unimaginable horror.

He hung on to hope that one day he might be able to see his wife again, who was taken to another concentration camp, and publish his work to help people survive different life traumas, including war. This is what gave his survival purpose and fueled his daily efforts not to succumb to the horror of suffering all around him.

Frankl made it out of the concentration camp alive, although sadly, his wife did not survive. He went on to establish a new branch of psychiatry called logotherapy, which helps people to live more fully and overcome challenges by connecting to their sense of meaning in life. *Man's Search for Meaning* has sold more than ten million copies and has inspired millions of people, including me.

By focusing on his purpose—to see his wife, to help others by sharing his work—Frankl built a Bridge of Resilience that helped him persevere until he and the other prisoners were freed. But his purpose wasn't something that happened to him or something that he was lucky to find. He made an *active choice* to keep his hope and sense of purpose alive by imagining himself giving lectures to help people survive the trauma of war and recounting the lines from the manuscript he had written for another book before he was captured.

In *Man's Search for Meaning*, Frankl writes, "Everything can be taken from a man but one thing: the last of the human freedoms—to choose one's attitude in any given set of circumstances, to choose one's own way."

If there was a single quote to describe the essence of what I hope you take away from your Awesome Human Project, it's this. Challenges, crises, difficulties, and dark moments are inevitable parts of life. **But you get to courageously *choose* your attitude toward the challenge, and when you boldly embrace it and actively search for positive meaning within it, you build a Bridge of Resilience that can help carry you through it.**

When I went through my burnout and the several years of rebuilding myself and my life afterward, at first I just tried to make it through each day. Making breakfast for my family, taking a walk, reading for a few minutes—these simple activities took all my motivation and energy. But as I began to heal, slowly, I started to get glimpses of how making it to the other side of my struggle could be meaningful. Without knowing any of this research about resilience, I sensed that having a purpose greater than "just make it through" would help me persevere through a really dark time.

NOTE TO SELF

You get to choose your attitude toward any challenge.

My daughter, Mia, gave me some of my earliest glimmers of hope and meaning. I wanted to be a great mom—to bring light, good energy, love, and care into Mia's life—without the heavy cloud of overwhelm and inner struggle. I also wanted to be a good role model for the relationship Mia was creating with herself. The only way I could do that was to cultivate a more supportive relationship with myself.

When I began to find the courage to openly share my struggles—something I'd never done before because super-women and forces of nature don't have struggles!—I found another source of meaning: hearing about my challenges and how I was working through them helped a lot of people! I was so nervous to talk about my burnout to all the members of my Happier community. But wow, if I ever needed a reminder that sharing your struggles doesn't make you weak but makes you an Awesome Human who can help a lot of people, I got it with confetti and fireworks.

So many people reached out to say that just by opening up, I was helping them to feel less alone in their struggles and have hope that they could find a way through them. This was so meaningful to me, and it fueled me to keep practicing my emotional fitness skills and to share what I was learning, including my stumbles and low moments. This sense of purpose became my Bridge of Resilience.

Here's a practice to build your own Bridge of Resilience this week.

PRACTICE

Build Your Bridge of Resilience

Begin by identifying a challenge you're working through or will need to work through soon. It can be big or small.

Then take a few moments to reflect on your answers to the questions below:

How does my working through this challenge help others in some way?

How does it contribute to a meaningful goal I have?

What can I learn that will help me grow and evolve in a meaningful way?

I highly recommend that you write down your answers because you'll be able to "hear" them more clearly.

Remember that your brain's negativity bias gets even more sensitive when you're going through something difficult, causing you more stress and anxiety. But when you practice your Bigger Why, you remind your brain that the stress and other difficult emotions you're experiencing have a purpose. You're not "just" stressed; you're stressed because you are doing something meaningful to you. Research shows that when you put your stress into this context, it becomes more manageable, and when you know that there is an endpoint—at some point you will do the challenging but meaningful thing and not feel stressed—it feels less overwhelming. This is how the Lens of the Bigger Why strengthens your resilience and helps you get through tough times.

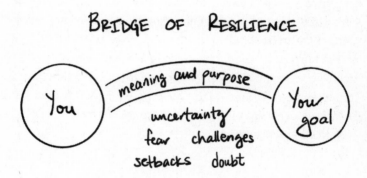

Your Bridge of Resilience Through Fear

Your Bigger Why can help you build another kind of Bridge of Resilience—through fear.

In chapter 4, about courage, I told you that one of my least favorite pieces of advice is to feel fearless. Fear is our brain's natural response to challenges. You can't get rid of fear, but you can grow your courage to be bigger than your fear by practicing your Bigger Why.

Here's the punch line: **your Bigger Why helps you get through fear because it shifts your brain's focus away from**

looking for danger and toward something that gives you meaning and purpose.

Remember that your brain's number one job is to protect you from danger. When you're doing something new or challenging, it gets really focused on finding that danger. The more your brain thinks about danger, the more fear you feel.

Imagine you're standing on the edge of a cliff and you need to jump to the other side (let's make this a somewhat scary but not unreasonable kind of jump). The more you look down from the cliff, the more danger your brain sees, and the more fear you have of falling and getting hurt or worse.

But imagine that your friend has already jumped to the other side, and she twisted her ankle when she landed on her feet. Of course, you want to help her! Now jumping to the other side isn't just about jumping but about helping your friend, something that's undoubtedly meaningful to you. Your brain is still afraid, but you have more courage to make the jump. By practicing your Bigger Why, you connected the scary action (jumping) to something meaningful (helping your friend), and that became your Bridge of Resilience Through Fear.

Here's a practice I want you to try.

PRACTICE

Bridge of Resilience Through Fear

Think of something you have to do—today, this week, soon—that's making you nervous or uncomfortable.

Step 1: Get honest about your fear.

Ask: *What am I actually afraid of?*

Your first answer will usually just scratch the surface, so after you have it, ask, *Why* does this scare me? and be specific in your answers.

Acknowledging your fear honestly and specifically will reduce its intensity (remember the science of acknowledging difficult feelings) and help you have more clarity for how your Bigger Why can help you through it.

Step 2: Build your Bridge of Resilience Through Fear.

Ask yourself: *How does doing this thing that scares me contribute to someone else or something greater than me, or help me work toward a meaningful goal?*

Be specific, and don't BS yourself here. Your Bridge of Resilience Through Fear will be stronger if your answer to this question is truly meaningful to you, not just something that sounds nice.

You've already had to do a lot of things that involve working through fear as part of your Awesome Human Project. Here are just a few:

- Talking back to your brain when it traps you in self-doubt

- Sharing what's on your Emotional Whiteboard with others

- Having difficult conversations

- Saying no to someone

Here's how you could use this practice to reframe each one to grow your courage bigger than your fear:

Fearful Thought	Bridge of Resilience
I'm not qualified for this job and get nervous during interviews, so I'm definitely not going to get it.	**Fear**: How I'll feel if I am rejected/how other people will react when I tell them I didn't get it **Reframe:** "Getting this job will help me grow and take the next important step in my career. By going for it, I am also encouraging people I care about to reach higher in their own careers."
People on my team will think I'm weak if I share with them that I'm struggling.	**Fear:** Being seen as weak by colleagues/not feeling supported when I share **Reframe:** "Everyone is struggling with something. When I open up, I help people on my team to feel less alone in their challenges and give them permission to feel that it's okay to not always feel okay."
I'm afraid to share this feedback with my colleague because she will get upset.	**Fear:** My colleague won't like me **Reframe:** "I'm sharing this feedback because I care about my colleague, and I want to help her improve."

	Fear: My friend won't like me, and she will stop asking me to go out
I'm exhausted, but I'm afraid to upset my friend if I tell her that I can't go out tonight.	**Reframe:** "It's important that I have enough energy for my family and my work tomorrow, and if I go out tonight, I'll be burned out. I'm sure my friend feels this way, too, sometimes, so she will understand if I'm honest."

One of the women who participated in our Elevating Women Leaders program recently reached out for advice. (She asked that I keep her name private.) She was up for a big promotion and had to write her self-evaluation, but her brain was overwhelming her with all kinds of stories about not being good enough for it. "I'm rage-writing my self-evaluation, and that's definitely not the energy I want to bring into it," she said.

"Your brain is afraid of what will happen if you don't get this promotion and also if you do get it because both of those scenarios introduce a lot of uncertainty and new challenges," I told her. "So it's trying to pull you back from so-called danger with self-doubt and not-good-enoughness. It's like it thinks that if it introduces enough doubt, you might give up this whole thing altogether and danger will be gone," I told her.

I asked her to have a meeting with her brain and acknowledge its fears, understanding that it's scared by both the worst-case (don't get the promotion) and the best-case (do get it) scenarios. "Think through each one, and remind your brain that you've done hard things, gotten over rejection, and adjusted to new positions before," I suggested.

Then I asked her to look at her self-evaluation through the Lens of the Bigger Why: to worry less about showing that she was good enough for the promotion and to think more about how getting this promotion would help her do what is most meaningful to her at work.

"I am an empathetic leader and care a lot about helping people on my team develop, connect, and grow. That's what I love to do! And we've talked a lot about how our company could benefit from having more empathetic leaders in senior positions," she said excitedly.

There it was: she had begun to build her Bridge of Resilience Through Fear of not being good enough by connecting how getting the promotion would help her team, her company, and its senior leadership. Her energy had changed—there were spunk and confidence in her voice. She went from "rage-writing" to "meaning-fueled writing." (I know you're dying to know: she got the promotion! But when I congratulated her, she told me that although she was thrilled about it, she was even prouder of being true to herself in her self-evaluation.)

Don't Let Too Much Bigger Why Lead You to Burnout

Practicing your Bigger Why to connect your daily activities and challenges to a sense of meaning is powerful. But there is such a thing as too much Bigger Why. And if you don't combine your practice of the Bigger Why with other emotional fitness skills, it can lead you to burnout.

This is actually a risk I face with my work. It took me more than forty years to get to a place where, for the first time in my life, I feel that the work I am doing is what I'm meant to do and the best way I can contribute to others. It's an incredible feeling.

But because I love my work so much and I feel such a great sense of purpose doing it, it's very easy for me to do it too much and burn myself out. And even though I'm aware of this, it happens more than I'd like. I get to this place where I know I am tired but I feel so compelled to make one more change to my talk to make it better, answer one more email from an Awesome

Human asking for advice. . . . My Bigger Why beats out my awareness that I am running low on energy, and I overcommit.

I've seen this happen to so many Awesome Humans, so please hear me on this:

Loving what you do doesn't mean you magically have unlimited energy to do it. You are a human being, so doing a lot makes you feel tired and drains your energy, and you need to intentionally fuel it. The Bigger Why is not a replacement for self-care.

And while we're on this topic, can we also just do a reality check and acknowledge that just because you love your work and find it meaningful doesn't mean that sometimes you don't:

feel like doing it.

get sick of it.

hate some parts of it.

feel completely unmotivated.

wish you were doing something else.

NOTE TO SELF

Just because you love your work doesn't mean that you have unlimited energy to do it.

You're an Awesome HUMAN; you can feel all kinds of different emotions, so please don't judge yourself if sometimes you want nothing to do with the work you really love. It would be really weird if that never happened!

I've never liked that expression: "If you love what you do, you won't work a day in your life." That's a recipe for burnout. Your work, however meaningful, requires a lot of your energy. And you need to intentionally and regularly fill your energy reservoir if you want to continue to do what's meaningful to you.

When you recognize this, you'll see that your self-care is your responsibility—to your work and the people you care about. Only by taking care of yourself can you truly honor that which is most meaningful in your life and bring your Awesome Human capacity to it.

Practices in This Chapter

Lens of the Bigger Why
To-Do List Makeover
Build Your Bridge of Resilience
Bridge of Resilience Through Fear

Your Note to Self

What is something you want to remember, practice, or reflect on from this chapter?

AWESOME HUMAN AWARD

After you've done the different Bigger Why practices and completed your week, proudly give yourself the **Uncovering My Bigger Why** award! This is a big one, and you've earned it!

You. Are. Awesome!

Woohoo! Congrats on finishing your Five-Week Emotional Fitness Challenge!

I'm really proud of you. No, seriously, I am. Learning and practicing these emotional fitness skills is not easy, and they take a lot of courage, commitment, and talking back to your brain.

And listen, I'm proud of you even if you didn't do all the practices, or if you're reading this after having completed just a few weeks of your challenge. You've made the courageous decision to begin to embrace your Awesome Human, and that's a huge step.

After you do complete the five weeks, I want you to give yourself the **I Rocked My Five-Week Emotional Fitness Challenge** award! If by chance you have some confetti lying around, throw it all over yourself to celebrate. Dancing around the room to some really loud music is the next most appropriate response.

Awesome Human Award

I rocked my 5 - week emotional fitness challenge!

So, now what? Are you done?

C'mon, you know what I'm going to say. More practice!

In the next part of your Awesome Human Project, you're going to learn how to make the qualities and skills you've begun to develop part of your daily life. And I've got some suggestions for how you can use them to work through tough challenges or when you get stuck in the Valley of Struggle.

Let's go!

PART IV

KEEP YOUR PRACTICE GOING

How to Be an Awesome Human **Every Day** . . . or **Most Days**, Anyway!

CHAPTER 14

Quick Tips for Regular Practice

Hopefully by this point you're getting sick of me reminding you to practice your Awesome Human Qualities and skills, so I'll skip giving you another TED Talk about the importance of regular practice. Instead, I want to give you some super-practical tips about *how* you can integrate what you've learned during your Awesome Human Project into your daily routine so you can keep the practice going.

You learned a focus practice for each skill, and I encourage you to practice it daily. To help you do this, I created a really simple Daily Emotional Fitness Workout that I love to do in the mornings and sometimes at night, especially if I've had a tough day. It brings all five focus practices together in a quick way and helps me to begin or end the day feeling more centered and clear, not stuck in the Valley of Struggle. Sometimes I combine this workout with my Daily Fuel-Up practice (you learned about it in chapter 11, on self-care), and if you have time to do that, I highly recommend it.

Here's how to do it.

PRACTICE

Daily Emotional Fitness Workout

If you journal, you might want to keep your notebook or device nearby so you can jot down some reflections, but that's totally up to you! As you get into the habit of doing this workout, you might find that you don't need to go through every question each time, or you might put the questions in your own words. Awesome—the ones I include below are just prompts to get you started.

Check In with Yourself

You always begin here, by taking a moment to check in with yourself. It's a really beautiful way to remind yourself every single day that you, your emotional fitness, and your well-being are important to you.

How do I feel right now?

What is written on my Emotional Whiteboard?

If you notice that you're stuck in the Valley of Struggle, practice Struggle Awareness next. If not, skip it and go to Acceptance.

Struggle Awareness

How might the way I am thinking about today/
something that's coming up/something that
happened cause me to struggle more?

How can I shift my thoughts to struggle less?

A great way to shift out of struggle is by practicing
Acceptance. So this is your next step.

Acceptance

How can I look at my day or a challenge I'm dealing
with through the Lens of Acceptance? Focus on
the facts versus stories my brain is telling me and
identify one thing I could do to move forward with
less struggle.

A reminder that accepting your difficult or
uncomfortable feelings is a really important part of
Acceptance. Don't slight it.

Next up is your Gratitude practice. If you're feeling especially down or stuck in a negative thought spiral, spend
a little more time on it.

Gratitude

Lens of Gratitude: What are three specific things or
people I am grateful for in this moment?

Don't forget to put yourself on your gratitude list,
especially if your self-critic is piping up.

Your Self-Care practice is next.

Self-Care

Lens of Self-Care: How is my emotional, mental, and physical energy reservoir right now?

What is something I can do to fuel my energy? (If you have time to do your Daily Fuel-Up as part of your workout, awesome, but if not, that's also okay! Just make a specific plan for when and how you will do it later today.)

What is something I could do less of today/tomorrow so it doesn't drain my energy? What is my specific plan for doing less of it? (E.g., put the phone away after 9 p.m. to reduce mindless social media scrolling.)

Next up, Intentional Kindness and the Bigger Why.

Intentional Kindness

Lens of Kindness: What is something kind I can do right now to connect with, elevate, or support another person? (E.g., text a friend to check in, write a note of gratitude to a colleague, give a hug to someone in your family—whatever feels right.)

If you're doing this workout at the end of your day, ask yourself: How was I kind or compassionate today?

Bigger Why

To-Do List Makeover: Look at your to-do list, and ask yourself how some of the things you did/will do contribute to others or toward a meaningful goal you have for yourself.

If you're dealing with a challenge, use your Bridge of Resilience and think about how working through this challenge is meaningful to you and how it might be of service to others.

At the end of your workout, say something supportive to yourself! Practice positive self-talk, and remember to use the second person or use your name for the most punch. You might even want to make up an Awesome Human Award for yourself! Just last week, as I was doing this workout at the end of a really tough day, I gave myself the **You Made It Through This Crazy Week and Didn't Run Away from Your Family!** award. (You're totally welcome to borrow this one anytime.)

The Awesome Human Checklist (a.k.a. Questions to Help You Practice Regularly)

Sometimes you need a quick reminder to practice your Awesome Human Qualities and skills, especially when your brain has dragged you into the Valley of Struggle, you're worn out, or you are feeling overwhelmed. The best way I've found to do this is to ask myself a simple question that acts like a lens: it helps to focus my attention on what I can do to struggle less, support myself, and move forward through whatever challenge I'm dealing with in the best way.

I've pulled together my favorite questions into a little checklist. All of them should be familiar to you after having done your Awesome Human Project.

The Awesome Human Checklist

☑ Is the way I'm thinking about this causing me to struggle more?

☑ Is this fueling or draining?

☑ Is this thought helpful?

☑ Am I treating myself as I would treat a friend?

☑ What is 1 thing I could do right now to move forward?

You can write these questions—or the ones that resonate the most!—on sticky notes or index cards and put them where you'll see them often. You can even put these on your calendar from time to time or schedule them as reminders to pop up on your phone.

Awesome Humans have sent me photos of their notes with these questions in their planners, stuck to bathroom mirrors, or on computer monitors. I love it, and I would love to see yours! (Tag me on Instagram @natalykogan or email me at natalyk@happier.com.)

One final note about practicing your Awesome Human Qualities and skills regularly:

BE KIND TO YOURSELF AND FORGET ABOUT PERFECTION!

Seriously. You're an Awesome Human, not a perfect human. Sometimes you'll get stuck in the Valley of Struggle or not feel like practicing. That's okay! Just get back to it when you can. The only thing that matters is that you do.

NOTE TO SELF

You are an Awesome human, not a machine. You are not supposed to get it right all the time.

CHAPTER 15

When You're Stuck in the Valley of Struggle

No matter how long you've been practicing your Awesome Human Qualities and skills, sometimes your brain finds a way to trap you in the Valley of Struggle anyway. I teach this stuff for a living, and it still happens to me!

When you realize that's happened, I want you to feel really awesome because you noticed! Becoming aware that you're stuck in the Valley of Struggle is huge because with awareness you give yourself an opportunity to get out of it.

When you become aware, practice your Struggle Awareness, and identify one way you could shift your thoughts to struggle less: 99 percent of the time, the way to struggle less is to practice Acceptance so you can separate the facts from the story your brain has made up, acknowledge your feelings and the situation with clarity, and identify one step you can take to move forward out of the Valley of Struggle.

Often that step will be to practice one of the other qualities or skills. For example, if you recognize that your brain's negativity bias has taken over and you're seeing only the downside of a situation, you might practice Gratitude to even out your perspective. Or if your inner critic is in overdrive, self-compassion and shifting to talking to yourself as you would to a friend is a great next step.

As you practice your Awesome Human Qualities and skills regularly, you will become better at knowing which ones you need to lean in to when you're struggling. Yep, that's another reason to practice regularly: consistent practice makes it easier to access the most helpful qualities and skills when times are tough and you really need them.

Here's a quick little guide you might find helpful. (I had to have a serious talk with my inner perfectionist, who tried to make me feel like crap for not drawing this entire illustration by hand. "But you drew all the other ones!!!" she yelled. "But what I really care about is making the illustrations clear and useful!" I said back, kindly but firmly. Always. Be. Practicing!)

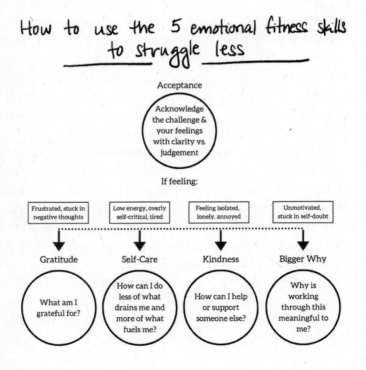

How to use the 5 emotional fitness skills to struggle less

Acceptance

Acknowledge the challenge & your feelings with clarity vs. judgement

If feeling:

Frustrated, stuck in negative thoughts	Low energy, overly self-critical, tired	Feeling isolated, lonely, annoyed	Unmotivated, stuck in self-doubt
Gratitude	Self-Care	Kindness	Bigger Why
What am I grateful for?	How can I do less of what drains me and more of what fuels me?	How can I help or support someone else?	Why is working through this meaningful to me?

SOS (a.k.a. Quick Help When You're Stuck)

Sometimes you just need help, and you need it ASAP.

So, in this section, I pulled together some of the most frequent ways we get stuck in the Valley of Struggle, and for each one, I wrote you a Note to Self to help you get out of it. I also point you to where in the book you can go to refresh Awesome Human Qualities, skills, and practices that will help you get unstuck.

I'd happily give you my cell number so you can text me an SOS whenever you get stuck, but then my family wouldn't like me very much. So think of this section as the closest possible thing. But the more you practice your Awesome Human Qualities and skills, the more you'll discover that you can answer your own SOS messages and get yourself out of the Valley of Struggle. (You can still email me anytime at natalyk@happier.com, including to tell me how you did it!)

Overwhelmed

I feel overwhelmed with work, life, and taking care of everyone—and I never have a moment for myself.

NOTE TO SELF

You can't give what you don't have.

Practicing self-care is an act of love toward the people you care about.

Review: Self-Compassion (p. 65), Self-Care (p. 185)
Practice: Lens of Self-Care (p. 190), Daily Fuel-Up (p. 208)

Stuck in Negative Thoughts

I'm always worried about what could go wrong and can't relax even when everything is okay.

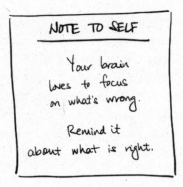

NOTE TO SELF

Your brain loves to focus on what's wrong.

Remind it about what is right.

Review: Courage to Talk Back to Your Brain (p. 47), Gratitude (p. 161)
Practice: Lens of Gratitude (p. 179), Talk Back to Your Brain (p. 60)

Can't Relax

*My brain won't let me rest, and I always feel like
I need to be busy doing something.*

NOTE TO SELF

Life is not a checklist.

Stop judging yourself
by the size
of your productive output.

Review: Self-Care (p. 185)
Practice: Daily Fuel-Up (p. 208), No/Yes Trade-Off (p. 196)

Stuck in "This Is Not How It Should Be"

*Nothing ever goes my way, and I get stuck in
"this is not how it should be!"*

NOTE TO SELF

You can always
choose to shift from
"this is not how it <u>should</u> be"
to
"what <u>could</u> I do given
how this is?"

Review: Acceptance (p. 131), Gratitude (p. 161)
Practice: Lens of Acceptance (p. 138), Gratitude Antidote (p. 171)

Don't Feel Good Enough

*I always feel like I'm not good enough (at my job,
at being a good friend, parent, etc.).*

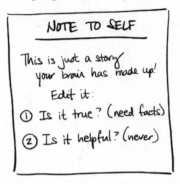

Review: Courage (p. 47), Self-Compassion (p. 65)
Practice: Edit Your Story (p. 53), Call BS on Your "Not Good Enough" (p. 79)

Burning Out from Overcommitting

*I'm burning out from overcommitting and saying yes, but I feel
so guilty about saying no and afraid to disappoint people!*

Review: Acceptance (p. 131), Self-Care (p. 185), Bigger Why (p. 241)
Practice: No/Yes Trade-Off (p. 196), Bridge of Resilience Through Fear (p. 256)

Drowning in Others' Negativity

My partner/friend/colleague is really negative, and their negativity is draining and frustrating.

NOTE TO SELF

You can't change others.
  But you can:
- respect your boundaries
- practice your joy
- fuel your energy
- practice compassion

Review: Intentional Kindness (p. 221), Self-Care (p. 185)
Practice: Lens of Compassion for Frustration (p. 237), How to Limit Energy Drain from Difficult People (p. 199)

Missing Joy

I feel no joy in my life—it's like I'm just going through the motions.

NOTE TO SELF

Practice your joy!
Make it a priority.
Joy is your life fuel
  and it deserves
your commitment.

Review: Gratitude (p. 161), Self-Care (p. 185)
Practice: Lens of Gratitude (p. 179), Create Your Temptation Bundle (p. 215)

Working Parent Guilt

I constantly feel guilty as a working parent. I feel guilty when I miss time with my kids for work; guilty about not being awesome at work; it's endless.

Review: Courage (p. 47), Self-Compassion (p. 65)
Practice: Talk Back to Your Brain (p. 60), Three Steps to Talking to Yourself Like a Friend (p. 74)

Endless Self-Criticism

I'm always criticizing myself, and I don't know how to stop—I hate the voice in my head.

Review: Courage (p. 47), Self-Compassion (p. 65), Gratitude (p. 161)
Practice: Edit Your Story (p. 53), Gratitude Swap (p. 176)

Embracing Your Awesome Human

You ARE an Awesome Human.

You aren't broken, and you don't need fixing.

You have so much goodness inside of you, and you have the capacity to bring it out so you can work and live with

NOTE TO SELF

You have so much awesomeness inside of you. Keep practicing bringing it out!

a greater sense of meaning, connection, and joy. Are you perfect? No way (no one would want that!). Do you have work to do, including a lot of talking back to your brain? Of course!

But that's all part of embracing your Awesome Human and practicing this skill we call living.

With this book, you began your Awesome Human Project. You've learned the mindset shifts, skills, and practices to empower you to bring your Awesome Human into every part of your work and life.

But just because you've reached the end of this book doesn't mean you're done. In fact, there is no end: **embracing your Awesome Human is a lifelong commitment.**

It's a commitment first and most importantly to yourself to create a more supportive relationship with yourself, your thoughts, your emotions, and other people so you can struggle less and thrive more.

It's a commitment to the work you care about because when you embrace your Awesome Human, you bring your full capacity and potential to everything you do.

It's a commitment to every single person you interact with because when you embrace your Awesome Human, you can be a force of good who helps *them* struggle less and thrive more.

I am honored to have been your guide as you built the foundation for your Awesome Human Project, but I'm not going anywhere. Because of the gift of technology, we can stay connected in many ways, including through social media. You can find all the ways to stay connected at the end of this chapter, but remember you can always email me at natalyk@happier.com—I would love to hear about your Awesome Human Project and what you're learning and discovering on your journey! (Yes, I really mean that; I love getting emails from Awesome Humans telling me about how they're practicing.)

And now I get to proudly, excitedly, and with all the fireworks and confetti you can imagine, give you the **Boldly, Courageously Embracing My Awesome Human** award!

Accept it proudly, and embrace it boldly, courageously, and compassionately.

You ARE an Awesome Human!

With love and gratitude,

Nataly, your fellow Awesome Human

Let's stay connected (thank you, technology!).

Sign up for my weekly email (I write every single one myself): happier.com

Follow me on Instagram, where I share (almost) daily: @natalykogan

Connect with me on Facebook: @natalykoganauthor, on LinkedIn/natalykogan or on Twitter: @natalykogan

Subscribe to my YouTube channel: @natalykoganhappier

And last but not least, join me for Awesome Human Hour, my weekly live show, and subscribe to my Awesome Human podcast! To get more info, just visit natalykogan.com.

I LOVE to speak to and do workshops with companies, teams, leaders, and all kinds of Awesome Humans. To inquire about booking me, please email speaking@happier.com.

If you're interested in our Happier @ Work program or the virtual leadership programs I lead, please email team@happier.com.

Oh, and to send me notes about your progress with your Awesome Human Project, digital confetti, or anything else you want to share, email natalyk@happier.com.

Your Very Own Awesome Human Award

One of the benefits I discovered as part of doing my own Awesome Human Project is that I became much better at supporting myself, pumping myself up when I need it, and celebrating big and small wins, something I rarely did before.

I hope that you, too, have become a more enthusiastic supporter of yourself throughout your Awesome Human Project. So for your last Awesome Human Award, I want you to create and give one to yourself!

What is something you're really proud to have learned or practiced?

How do you want to honor yourself for doing your inner work to chisel out and embrace your Awesome Human?

Think about these questions and then give yourself your very own Awesome Human award! Have some fun with it, and think about doing it regularly, not just this once!

MY AWESOME HUMAN AWARD

I'm an Awesome Human because _____

_____

_____

_____

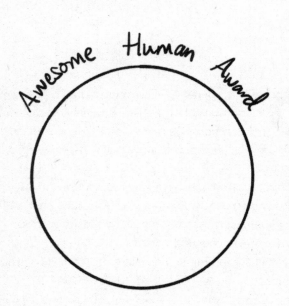

I give myself the _____

_____

_____

award and I unabashedly, excitedly, and boldly embrace it!

You Are Enough (a poem)

One evening, as I was finishing editing this book you're now holding, I realized I was exhausted, overworked, and yet still pushing myself to keep going.

I paused and was grateful that I noticed. Awareness is freaking powerful, right?

And then I started to write a Note to Self, to remind myself that I didn't have to earn my worth by always doing more, better, faster. My Note to Self grew into a little poem I wrote for all of us. I couldn't think of a better way to end this book than by sharing it with you.

YOU ARE ENOUGH

Maybe today you've done enough

And can rest

Even if you haven't hacked your Inbox to zero

Maybe today you can give less than 150%

And not feel bad

Even if everyone else is "grinding it out"

Maybe today you can just love yourself

Without having to be anything more

Even if the world screams at you to find your best self

Maybe today you can be grateful

For all that you have

Even if it's not all you've ever wanted

Maybe today you can practice your joy

And love every moment

Even if it's not productive

Maybe today

You can be enough

Because you are.

Gratitudes

To every Awesome Human who has come to my talks and Happier @ Work workshops—in person or virtually!—joined my weekly Awesome Human Hour, participated in our Leading Through Adversity, Elevating Women Leaders, and No-Guilt Self-Care programs, read my first book, *Happier Now*, my weekly emails and (so many!) social media posts, and watched my YouTube videos and pep talks: I AM SO GRATEFUL FOR YOU!!! You are a HUGE part of this book, and your notes, comments, and questions have been invaluable in helping me to clarify my ideas, make them better, and bring them to life. You have taught me so much, and you are my Bigger Why to keep teaching, speaking, and writing, even at times when my brain tells me all kinds of stories to get me to stop.

This isn't just my Awesome Human Project—it's OURS, together.

I'm immensely grateful to my dear friend and publisher Jaime Schwalb for being an invaluable partner in creating this book, and to the whole team at Sounds True for your commitment, hard work, and brilliance. I am proud and grateful to call Sounds True my author home.

Janis Donnaud, my fearless agent, thank you for always having my back—lucky me to have you in my corner.

To my speaking agents, first at the Harry Walker Agency and now at SpeakersOffice: Thank you for your hard work and dedication to helping me get in front of as many Awesome Humans as possible so I can help them struggle less and thrive more. Speaking is my love language, and I couldn't do it without you.

This book is a breakthrough, a kind of a personal revolution. I had to fight hard to get to a place where I felt I could bring the best of me to write the best possible book. And it wouldn't be possible without Claudia Boutote, who helped me bust through my inner walls with her warm and brilliant guidance. I am so incredibly grateful for you and think every author should have a Claudia to fight their revolution.

Buzzy Jackson, my most awesome editor: I am so grateful for your energy, wisdom, care, and utter confidence in my ability to do the doing. Great books need great editors, and awesome books need a Buzzy.

Debbie Karch, my partner in all things Happier and beyond: Thank you for you. For always seeing what's possible; for expanding, elevating, and bettering everything we do; for being up for all (okay, almost all) of my wild creative ideas; and for the care and love that you bring to every single Awesome Human we work with. And to me.

To my Avi, who has walked this path next to me for twenty-four years: Thank you for always believing in me, even when I couldn't believe in myself, and for making every small win feel like fireworks. Thank you for being my most engaged student and being so willing not just to hear my ideas but also to practice and share them with so many others. I am so grateful for you and for our weekend walks, during which many seeds that became parts of this book were planted.

My Mia, my love, you are my greatest teacher, light, and

inspiration—for this book and every book, talk, and living the practices I share here. To see you embrace so much of your Awesome Human and to know that I've somehow helped (or didn't get in the way!) is an honor. Thank you for being the best joiner and together with Avi, wrapping me in your love, care, and laughter. You two Awesome Humans built a cocoon within which I could find the courage to create my bravest and boldest project to date. Our trio and each of you are my greatest blessings. I love you beyond words.

And to my parents: Thank you for being and for your courage to take the journey to bring us all here thirty-two years ago. I don't take a single day for granted.

Finally, to you, the reader: Thank you for trusting me with your time, attention, and effort. It means a lot, and please know—I am rooting for you!

About the Author

Nataly Kogan is a leading global expert in optimizing your emotional fitness and elevating your leadership.

She's the creator of the Happier Method™, founder and CEO of Happier and Happier @ Work™, and author of Happier Now, Gratitude Daily, and The Awesome Human Project.

Nataly is a highly-sought after international keynote and TEDx speaker who has appeared in hundreds of media outlets, including *The New York Times*, *The Wall Street Journal*, and *The Washington Post*.

After years of chasing a non-existent state of nirvana in the corporate and startup worlds, Nataly was not only unfulfilled, she suffered a debilitating burnout that led her to find a new way to live and work. Today, she helps hundreds of thousands of people struggle less and thrive more through speaking, Happier @ Work training programs, virtual leadership programs, online courses, and her books.

Nataly came to the US as a refugee with her family when she was thirteen years old, and one of her greatest accomplishments was learning how to speak English by watching Alyssa Milano on the classic 80s sitcom, *Who's The Boss?*

Nataly lives outside of Boston with her husband and daughter, and when she isn't speaking or teaching, can be found painting colorful abstract art and cooking up a storm in her kitchen.

To bring Nataly to your company or organization, please email speaking@happier.com.

Please visit natalykogan.com to sign up for Nataly's awesome weekly email, register to attend Awesome Human Hour Live, and get tons of other super helpful resources to help fuel your Awesome Human Project!

About the Cover

When I saw the cover design for *The Awesome Human Project*, I was overwhelmed with excitement! I absolutely loved it and felt that it captured the energy and the essence of this book in the most perfect way.

But what brought me close to tears was seeing my art incorporated into the cover. Peeking out through the letters is a watercolor painting I'd painted during the summer when I began to write the book.

In the chapter on Self-Care, I shared my artist journey with you and how I went from denying myself the permission to paint because it was "a luxury and a waste of time" to painting because it brings me joy. My brain still likes to pipe up with stories of how "I'm not a real artist and not good enough"—of course I talk back to it!—so to see my own art on the cover of this book . . . well, it was a huge life moment for me.

I hope it fuels you, I hope you love it, and I want to tell you that it's called "The Lens of Gratitude." That's what I set out to paint and I love that it's the painting my publisher chose for the cover design without knowing its title and choosing from dozens of my possible artworks!

Parts of the painting have also been incorporated into the interior design of the book and the black and white version below. If you want to see it in full color, head over to natalykogan.com (you'll find more of my art there, too!).

About Sounds True

Sounds True is a multimedia publisher whose mission is to inspire and support personal transformation and spiritual awakening. Founded in 1985 and located in Boulder, Colorado, we work with many of the leading spiritual teachers, thinkers, healers, and visionary artists of our time. We strive with every title to preserve the essential "living wisdom" of the author or artist. It is our goal to create products that not only provide information to a reader or listener but also embody the quality of a wisdom transmission.

For those seeking genuine transformation, Sounds True is your trusted partner. At SoundsTrue.com you will find a wealth of free resources to support your journey, including exclusive weekly audio interviews, free downloads, interactive learning tools, and other special savings on all our titles.

To learn more, please visit SoundsTrue.com/freegifts or call us toll-free at 800.333.9185.

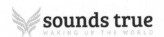

sounds true
WAKING UP THE WORLD

FIC
TRE

Trevino, Elizabeth
Borton de.

11598

I, Juan de Pareja

$9.26

DATE DUE	BORROWER'S NAME	ROOM NO.
MAR. 1 3 1997	Melody M.	7th
SEP 1 5 1999	Erica R.	8th

DATE DUE	BORROWER'S NAME	ROOM NO.